W9-BRF-841

The Merchants of Fear

Why *they* want us to be afraid...

Christopher Catherwood
and Joseph DiVanna

THE LYONS PRESS
Guilford, Connecticut
An imprint of The Globe Pequot Press

To buy books in quantity for corporate use
or incentives, call **(800) 962–0973**
or e-mail **premiums@GlobePequot.com**.

Copyright © 2008 by Christopher Catherwood and Joe DiVanna

ALL RIGHTS RESERVED. No part of this book may be reproduced or transmitted in any form by any means, electronic or mechanical, including photocopying and recording, or by any information storage and retrieval system, except as may be expressly permitted in writing from the publisher. Requests for permission should be addressed to The Globe Pequot Press, Attn: Rights and Permissions Department, P.O. Box 480, Guilford CT 06437.

The Lyons Press is an imprint of The Globe Pequot Press.

Text design by Sheryl P. Kober

Library of Congress Cataloging-in-Publication Data is available on file.

ISBN 978-1-59921-281-4

Printed in the United States of America

10 9 8 7 6 5 4 3 2 1

To my sons Frank and Leo,
in hopes that the world in which they live
will be a kinder, gentler place,
and to my wife Isabel,
for being there when I need her.

—Joe

To my wonderful Paulette,
without whom I could never write—
with fondest love from
an eternally grateful

—Christopher

THIS BOOK CHARACTERIZES THE UNITED STATES AS A NATION
with an economic problem: Capitalism's voracious appetite for
growth demands that consumers, business and government maintain a continuous rate of spending to ensure economic momentum.
To grow the American economy must continually seek out new customers, markets, and raw materials to maintain economic superiority and to secure its place in global markets. Is the U.S. economy's
need for growth sustainable or does the economy depend on periodic stimulation by geopolitical conflict? Perhaps more importantly,
if the world became a peaceful place could Americans continue to
live far beyond their means in the world's wealthiest debtor nation?
Does the U.S. need a common enemy to maintain financial activity, *MIC*
government spending, and economic growth, a notable factor that
can be found in several periods of U.S. history? Does the American *exeptionalism*
psyche fundamentally depend on having a common enemy to fear?
The book argues that the expansion of U.S. corporate global business trade and industry activity is predicated on the U.S. having a
common enemy to galvanize social thinking into spending toward
a greater good. At one time this was manifest as the conquest over
the evil of communism; today, that evil is terrorism. Terrorism has *crusades*
simply filled the void created by the end of the Cold War and the
decline in communism as a perceived threat. The U.S. consumer's
love affair with the automobile is a personification of the American
ideal of freedom. Automobiles depend on oil, thus oil is a strategic
resource whose supply must be maintained at a price affordable to
the average citizen. The quest for oil and other resources are but one
factor used to justify military activities cloaked under the ideals of
patriotism which are designed to maintain the American economy.

This book raises the following questions: Is there an alternative to America's need for a continual opposing force? How can

the U.S. play a more proactive role in global development? What is the relationship between the erosion of freedom and surrendering to fear in today's American society—and how can U.S. citizens become more aware of this dichotomy and its consequences to U.S. politics, economy, and culture? Six years after 9/11, Americans must ask themselves: Are we any safer now, or are we simply more aware of being afraid?

Contents

Contents

List of Figures

Preface

SINCE THE FOUNDING OF THE NATION, THE ECONOMIC ETHOS of the United States has been constructed on the rhetoric of freedom and the spread of democracy, which in turn has become part of the American psyche. From the palm of Adam Smith's invisible hand springs the ideals of a free market economy which it can be argued is the foundation for American entrepeneurism. U.S. citizens are proud to live in a free, democratic society, and often castigate other nations' political structures that do not reflect similar ideological constructs. Sometimes, condemnation is not enough, and direct action and indirect subversion against another nation takes place. The ideology of democracy and preservation of free-market capitalism have been key factors in the construction of a U.S. foreign policy based on interventions designed solely to promote, protect, and defend American financial interests.

There are three main reasons for U.S. foreign intervention: to realize political ambitions often cloaked under an umbrella of nationalism; to counter previously established aggressive regimes which seem to pose a threat (real or imagined) disguised by patriotism; and, perhaps more frequently, to support an agenda which feeds the voracious need for growth required to maintain the economic engine of U.S. capitalism. As a people, Americans often express concerns over other nation-states which are not democratic, and where censorship, torture, and suppression of basic human freedoms prevail. These concerns are repeatedly magnified by the media, and over time they have become key ingredients in national politics and military actions. During the second half of the twentieth century the media and the government have developed a symbiotic relationship using fear as a means to promote ratings and capture the eyes of more viewers while surreptitiously using fear as a means to justify political agendas and legitimize military actions. However, the role of the media has changed over the past few decades, acting now to promote its own agenda of fear, abandoning the work ethic of previous generations whose journalistic ideals involved reporting without fear or favour. The resolve that humankind should enjoy life, liberty, and the pursuit of happiness is the strength of the American character, and the use of fear to implement these ideals as a means to promote U.S. special economic interest is the failure of its foreign policies.

Americans take enormous pride in their democratic free-market version of capitalism, which acts as the underpinning of their success as a nation-state and a global economic power. During the twentieth century many nations aspired to the American achievement which resulted in the U.S. dollar evolving into the world's reserve currency. Achieving economic dominion over the world economy, America has actualized the characteristics of empire in all but in name. Few Americans consider the impact their economic achievement has on people of other nation-states, or how America is perceived by people in distant lands. As the self-declared bastion of all that is economically good, political parties on both sides of the congressional aisle typically find consensus when confronted with global impairments to America's economic success. Equally, political leaders become galvanized against the actions of other nations that do not share economic ideals that work to support U.S. economic or political objectives. Traditionally, the U.S. has waited for economic threats to manifest themselves before taking action. Now, under neoconservative doctrine, the United States prefers preemptive intervention, and no longer waits for events to unfold or enemies to manifest themselves. Simply, if the U.S. thinks you might be up to something that is detrimental to the future or current economic welfare of America, you move from an ally to the new list of emerging enemies. One could argue that the economic needs of the nation, such as the demand for raw materials, has moved from a simple element in the policy-making process to the driving force behind much of U.S. foreign policy.

During the long history of the U.S., the economic needs of the nation have been served by a foreign policy constructed to promote U.S. interests abroad. Fear has always been a ready tool of government to manipulate public opinion in the same way that business uses fear to sell products. Businesses know how to capitalize on fear, such as the insurance industry selling terrorism insurance to people who, if they consulted the actuarial tables to see the probability of a terrorist incident happening to them, would never take out a policy. The sharp rise in revenues of the industry now dedicated to security (personal, business and national) is a testament to a nation living under a shadow of fear. What is new in the twenty-first century is the growing incestuous relationship between business, government, and the media, and their increasing use of fear to justify their activities. The intent of this book is to explore the symbiotic relationship between these three elements of society and to understand the long-term implications of using fear as a mechanism to forge national policies and the consequential erosion on the value proposition of the United States in world markets. What is meant by *value proposition* is the sum of the total benefits which the U.S. brings to world markets and the perceived value of American goods and services to global consumers. In short, we examined the international role of the United States as an economic engine and how the growing fear of terrorism affects this role. Moreover, the book will focus on the psyche of the American people, examining the roots of fear in the U.S. as well as in other societies which now have a relationship with the U.S., to understand that the merchants of fear are only effective if they find the right buyers.

We would like to express that this book does not in any way condone, support, or applaud terrorism, nor does it seek to justify the actions of terrorists. Rather, the object of the book is to point out two key aspects of terrorism in the context of global, sociopolitical, and economic evolution. First, we address the effectivity of terrorism from the perspective of total return on investment, a financial viewpoint which many Americans may not be aware of, but can readily digest; and, second, we examine terrorism as an effective means to alter international trade, economics, and other aspects of global society due to the failure of the foreign policies of nation-states such as the U.S. to address the root cause of terrorist activities. Until the root causes of terrorism are addressed, actions to prevent terrorism through a process of preemptive interventions is the same as trying to cure cancer with magic beans. The third goal of this text is to examine the shortcomings of the U.S. reaction to terrorism by policy makers and the inability of U.S. citizens to comprehend the cause and effect of their personal behaviors and habits on the world theater.

To be controversial, one could argue that the acts of terrorism devised to promote a political agenda are the ultimate expression of freedom, as non-state actors try to reshape the world with far fewer resources than established sovereign nation-states. Are terrorists merely individuals acting beyond the constraints of accepted behavior established by society? Perhaps a more-controversial question would be, Are today's attitudes toward terrorists reminiscent of the British military assessment of the early American colonists' failure to fight by the rules of engagement? The British complained vehemently as the colonists concealed themselves behind trees and stone walls in New England in the 1770s, unlike the British soldiers who stood in splendid ranks. The failure to follow the rules of engagement, and actions like the Boston Tea Party, were considered acts of terrorism by the British monarchy. Just as in the past, today's terrorists act unencumbered by established laws, and therefore they are free to strike when, where, and how they please. Nevertheless, these actions, regardless of their purpose, are not to be admired, condoned, or promoted because they in turn violate the unwritten social contract between the people living in a free society and compromise the liberty of others. This raises the question: How can freedom and the demands of a free market economy be maintained internally within a nation and with other sovereign states without compromising the liberty, rights, and freedom of others?

This book argues that one of the driving factors of America's free market growth-based economy is a condition by which there is a continual need for a common enemy to justify spending and ratify political actions. Fear is the mechanism that acts as an agent to stimulate society to meet threats posed by enemies, both foreign and domestic, real and imagined. Here we will examine how businesses use fear to sell products; how the media foments fear to improve ratings and profits; and how the government appeals to fear to maintain spending levels. Terrorism is portrayed here as the latest replacement for the threat posed by the Cold War. The nation of free citizens that is America is unable to contemplate how to survive economically during a lasting peace. Government policy makers, the media, and business, each with their own objectives, conspire to a

military- Keynesianism [handwritten margin note]

smaller or larger extent depending on the circumstances to perpetu-
ate fear as a mechanism to stimulate economic activity.

Orchestrated socioeconomic activities—such as President John F.
Kennedy's race to space as a response to the fear of the USSR achieving a strategic advantage over America—is another example of this
principle. Defense spending acts as the catalyst to fuel the engine of
the U.S. industrial military complex, encouraging economic stability
in the U.S. while creating instability in other parts of the world. As
the U.S. consumer market becomes saturated, expansion into global
markets is the only avenue available to keep the economic engine
of American capitalism from collapsing in on itself. Without digress-
ing into a philosophical debate, one could argue that the difference
between the U.S. economy under capitalism and the former Soviet
Union's economy under communism is that the Soviet economy lost
its momentum and simply ran out of money first.

Meanwhile, American businesses use fear in two distinctly
different ways: to convince consumers to buy products, and to
influence policy makers to construct trade agreements that act
as protectionism, strictly to preserve U.S. interests. The third use
of fear comes from the free press, who provides the stimulation
for government objectives and business activity by perpetuating
fear into almost every aspect of American life. Television and print
media focus on sensationalism, targeting the extreme dimensions
of an event and delivering a modern-day version of David and
Goliath. Today's news media focuses on reporting the event as it
happens, without exploring the cause and effect in a global context. A protest of fifty people in a distant land is filmed close-up to
appear larger than life providing any small special interest group
with a global broadcast of its message at no cost. Hollywood has
reinforced the need for fear over the last half-century by providing

ready-made enemies: the Germans after World War II; communists in the '50s; the Russians during the Cold War; space aliens during the '90s; and now, in the twenty-first century, terrorists and the evils of global warming.

In the first three parts of this book, we will attempt to show how Americans have, over a number of centuries, come to develop their idea of freedom-based democratic capitalism, and how fear has now evolved into a fundamental part of the U.S. economic consciousness—or perhaps more appropriately, subconsciousness. In order to do this, we will not belabor post-9/11 events; instead, our intent is to concentrate on identifying social, cultural, and economic trends within specific events in U.S. history, such as the Independence period, the formation of the nation-state, nineteenth-century urbanism, McCarthyism, the Cold War, and more recent times. The objective of this debate is to place into a historical context the current reaction to terrorism in political, economic, and cultural perspectives. It is our aim to offer a reassessment of the value proposition of the United States to its citizens, as well as to the rest of the world, considering how much of this value proposition is based on the idea of a free nation, and what will happen if the nation continues to build on the fears of U.S. citizens.

In the fourth section, we will use historical data-points to project possible consequences of the American reaction to terrorism and its employment of fear as a mechanism for economic objectives. The goal of this final part is not to predict or foretell the eventual decline or dissipation of the American economic empire, but to point out the causal relationship between U.S. national objectives and international redress.

Acknowledgments

I WOULD LIKE TO EXPRESS MY DEEPEST THANKS TO MY COAUTHOR, Christopher Catherwood, for his patience and perseverance during the life of this manuscript. I proposed the idea for this book to him in 2003 over coffee, after attending his lectures on *Why the Nations Rage: Killing in the Name of God* at the University of Cambridge. When we submitted our book proposal to publishers, it was initially met with a negative reaction. Publishers felt that American readers would not be receptive to open criticism; however, Christopher's diligence in revisiting the subject with publishers led to The Lyons Press bringing this manuscript to the light of day. In addition, a great amount of appreciation is owed to Ronnie Gramazio at The Lyons Press for his understanding as we pieced together and consolidated four years of research into a very short book. A heartfelt thank you is due to Alison Picard our literary agent in the U.S. whose diligence found a home for this manuscript.

During the course of writing this book I have met and discussed the subject with many people in the United Kingdom, Ireland, France, the United Arab Emirates, Qatar, Bahrain, Saudi Arabia, Egypt, Jordan, Pakistan, South Africa, and the United States. It would be impossible to recognize all of them here, but I want them to know how much their interactions have helped to shape my thinking.

I would be remiss if I didn't extend a personal thank you to several people with whom I have had in-depth discussions. Over the years, Martin Dolan from CR2, a Dubai-based technology firm, has constantly served as a good sounding board for my ideas; his ability to synthesize my thoughts in a Middle Eastern context has always been helpful in forcing me to see both sides of the issues in that region. Yan Senouf, an attorney who lives just a few blocks from Ground Zero in New York, provided me with insight into how Americans have been reacting to global events in a post-9/11 world. Senouf's perspective often challenged my preconceived notions about what America is thinking.

An additional thank you must be said to Stephen Timewell, Editor-in-Chief of *The Banker* magazine in London, who has been instrumental in challenging me to examine the macroeconomic implications of U.S. policy in the Middle East. Jay Rogers, a management consultant in Boston, a longtime friend and confidant, was influential in helping me to understand the liberal-versus-conservative perspective on many issues. Waleed Sadek from Visa International-Egypt has also provided me with an understanding of many issues from the perspective of what young people are thinking in the Middle East, which helped immensely in rethinking my opinions on Islam.

As always, I am grateful to the fellows of King's College, Cambridge, for their constant support and access to resources during my ongoing research on global issues.

Perhaps most important, I owe a large debt of gratitude to my wife, Dr. Isabel DiVanna, who steadfastly reads my text and challenges my ideas while finishing her second PhD, watching our son Leo, and doing a variety of jobs which would make the busiest CEO's head spin. Isabel's perspective as a Brazilian citizen, one who lived in fear of a civil war for twenty years of her life, was extremely helpful as I worked to understand how societies react to enemies, both from within and without.

—Joseph A. DiVanna
Cambridge, June 2007

I AM FIRST OF ALL GRATEFUL TO MY FELLOW AUTHOR, JOE DiVANNA, for developing the concept for this book after attending my lectures on *Why the Nations Rage: Killing in the Name of God.* Joe's enthusiasm and inspiration kept this project alive and led to its fruition. I wish to proclaim four cheers for Joe DiVanna, and for his wife Isabel and son Leo, whose entire life so far has paralleled the writing of this book.

Second, I must thank my wonderful and ever-supportive wife, Dr. Paulette Catherwood, who teaches at the ACE Centre of the Cambridge University Institute of Continuing Studies. She is my constant companion, muse, helpmeet, and far more besides, without whom I would never write a word. My thanks to her are lifelong and profound.

Much of this book has been written in the loft of the fifteenth-century part of my parents' home in Balsham, a village just outside Cambridge. This has been a most convivial place to work, and I am more than grateful to them.

I have also carried out much of the research at the University of Richmond, in Virginia, where I have had the great honor of being a Writer in Residence in the History Department, and a visiting professor at the School of Continuing Studies annual summer school. If I included a complete list of people to thank here, it would run on for many pages, but let me offer special gratitude to the excellent staff of the History Department, School of Continuing Studies, Osher Institute, International Education, Information Services, Boatwright Library, and, last but not least, to the University Bookstore and lunchtime services staff, who make the campus a real home away from home, especially when my wife is still in England.

During the actual writing I have been a key supervisor at Homerton College in Cambridge, and warmest thanks go to Steve

Watts for giving me such great pupils to teach during the 2006–2007 academic year. Many thanks also go to my many delightful colleagues at St. Edmund's College, Cambridge, and to Geoffrey and Janice Williams of the INSTEP program, which brings pupils from Tulane, Wake Forest, Rice, Villanova, and other similar American institutions to Cambridge each year.

Many thanks also go to the ever-helpful staff at Heffers in Cambridge, especially Bruce Dixon and Richard Reynolds, for finding so many invaluable books to aid in my research. Richard and his wife Sally are part, along with my wife, of my great Wednesday support group, to whom much gratitude is also due, along with similar friends who correspond by e-mail from as far afield as the U.S. and Ethiopia.

Joe will have thanked the agent for this project, Alison Picard, and I must thank my own agents, Frank Weimann and Jaimee Garbacik, for allowing me time away from my major project, *Churchill: The True Story*, to write this book with Joe. Joe has thanked our splendid editor at The Lyons Press, so let me add my profound thanks to that company's legendary publisher, Gene Brissie. Gene was once my agent, when he owned James Peters Associates, and it is thanks very much indeed to him that my first international best-seller, *Churchill's Folly*, was written, and my subsequent literary career made possible. Working on another title with Gene has been a pleasure.

This is the first contracted book I have written after the death of my father-in-law, Reverend John S. Moore. He may no longer be with us, but he lived a very full eighty-seven years—in fact, most of the period covered by this book. He shared his personal memories of this era with me before he died, and his insights were incomparable. He is sorely missed and most fondly remembered.

—Christopher Catherwood
Cambridge, June 2007

Introduction: A Nation at the Crossroads of Freedom

*Insanity in individuals is something rare—but in groups, parties,
nations and epochs, it is the rule.*
—Friedrich Nietzsche

IN CIVILIZED SOCIETIES, THE ROLE OF THE STATE IS TO PROVIDE social cohesion to enable people to live together. In *The Republic*, Cicero remarks that the Free State is built on reciprocated bonds of affection between its citizens, one which can be broken by fear. These cohesive bonds can be called the fabric of society. When fear circumvents these bonds and the fabric of society is torn, people will look toward a centralized authority to reestablish social order.

Leaders throughout history have understood the relationship between fear and security. More important, leaders have understood all too well how to use fear as a key tool in shaping the attitudes of society. In 1932, Adolf Hitler said:

> *The streets of our country are in turmoil. The universities are filled with students rebelling and rioting. Communists are seeking to destroy our country. Russia is threatening us with her might, and the Republic is in danger. Yes—danger from within and without. We need law and order! Without it our nation cannot survive.*

Hitler understood that when fear becomes an obsession, the population will in turn look to a strong leader regardless of his/her political agenda. However, simply supplying fear is not enough; the fear must be presented (or packaged) in a way that instills a sense of urgency; as George Orwell remarked, leaders must first create an enemy to strike fear into the hearts of the electorate. The early-twentieth-century American social critic H. L. Mencken also noted that "[t]he whole aim of practical politics is to keep the populace alarmed—and hence clamorous to be led to safety—by menacing it with an endless series of hobgoblins, all of them imaginary." For the generation that grew up in the 1950s and 1960s under the specter of nuclear annihilation today's search for nations with weapons of mass destruction is a continuance of the same fear of death by nuclear exchange.

No matter how safe one may feel, fear is always just under the surface of our social bonds. Society, or at least our understanding of what it means to be civil, is protected by a thin veneer of rules, represented by laws (mostly unwritten) that govern our behavior. Just how fragile is the fabric of society? In reality, that which constitutes civility within any given group of people is a relatively flimsy facade of social behavior. In the immediate aftermath of Hurricane Katrina in New Orleans, people regressed to primitive levels of self-preservation in order to counter the perception of complete chaos. Although the media coverage of the event preyed on the extremes of the situation facing the city, one thing was evident: When people's fears are realized, the social fabric decays rapidly.

In the 1918 novel, *The Father of a Soldier*, William James Dawson wrote:

> *Those who say that fear lies at the root of all that is base in human life are undoubtedly right. The thief fears poverty, and*

therefore steals. The businessman fears defeat, and therefore stoops to dishonour. The thinker fears the ostracism which is the punishment of originality, and therefore hides his real convictions. We all fear pain, loss, and suffering, and therefore are willing to do almost everything to evade them. Most people fear Death, because they conceive it to mean the ultimate disaster. I returned from London in 1914 with fear for my companion. It was a sort of subtle ghost which manifested itself capriciously, disappearing for long intervals, reappearing unexpectedly, but, as I knew, never very far away.[1]

[handwritten margin note: fear + the logic of anarchy]

The real question is: Can fear lead to any good? In this case, can a society and a nation operating under the principle of fear (consciously or subconsciously) achieve progress? In the case of America, why has fear become such a powerful influence after 9/11?

American competitiveness had been in slow decline since the 1970s due to many factors: a natural erosion of the artificially high percentage of global market share acquired immediately after World War II; a shift from manufacturing to a service economy; an excessive value of the dollar against other currencies; inefficient management practices; and the government's reluctance to promote effective industrial policies.[2] One could argue that perhaps the events of 9/11 were instrumental in countering the most recent decline of the U.S. economy, caused first by the untold billions of U.S. dollars spent to fix the millennium computer problem (a fear that the world's computers would shut down or miscalculate at midnight January 1, 2000), and later, by the crash of the dot com/technology corporations. These issues were compounded by the citizens' demand to reduce military spending (the delayed peace dividend), and the tarnished space program. One has to consider the significant boost in corporate sales in the aftermath of 9/11, represented in the sudden surge of spending on security at home. This stimulated job growth in the security industry, and added to the increase in defense spending. Moreover, the U.S. reaction to these events was predictable, following the same patterns of patriotic rhetoric and reactionary legislation exhibited during McCarthy's hunt for communists in the post–World War II era.

This book offers an analysis of the ways in which fear has been used in the U.S. as an instrument to manipulate public opinion, justify public spending, and stimulate economic growth. More important, we show how fear of external subversive factions such as immigrants, communists, and now, terrorists, has had a long-standing role in the U.S. economic, societal, and political history. From a historical perspective, fear has become a way to sway social interests by the media, sell products by American business, and justify government spending by politicians and the periodic defense-led expansionism by the military.

Using fear as a tool is not simply creating a piece of propaganda; fear is a process of legitimization, exclusion, and prescribed interpretation.[3] To maintain economic growth based on the fear/threat principle, one must identify or create a common enemy with a clear and present danger. This theory is presented by William Blum, author of *Rogue State: A Guide to the World's Only Superpower*, who argues that the U.S. actually needs enemies to justify budgets and protect jobs. In short, an enemy acts to galvanize American society to a purpose or mission: "America cherishes her enemies. Without enemies, she is a nation without purpose and direction."[4] Just as American corporations need competitors to sustain business activities, so does the American economy need an enemy (real or imagined) to sustain or justify spending on defense.

Following the economic decline of America's longest-standing adversary, the Soviet Union, and the end of the Cold War, America's newest enemy is global terrorism, in any form, from any source, in any location. To ensure that terrorism is perceived as a larger-than-life threat and to fill the void left by the former USSR, the definition of terrorism required the broadest possible description so counterterrorism actions could be applied liberally to the widest possible number of unknown enemies and to a myriad of economic scenarios. The vague definition of terrorist acts in legislation such as the Patriot Act gives the government enormous latitude in classifying who is an enemy, from foreign factions like Middle East extremists, drug dealers, and governments that are not aligned with America's economic agenda to domestic troublemakers like illegal immigrants or local extremist groups. The express use of fear to achieve the goals of business, government, and the media places us directly in the cauldron of an immensely complex set of socioeconomic, political, and historical interpretations. To explore this line of thinking, we use a methodology of first developing a macro view of the issues, and then subsequently addressing each issue under three broad headings: the historical use of fear and its relationship to U.S. consumers; the national reaction to fear with consequences to U.S. foreign and domestic policies; and an analysis of the short- and long-term implications of U.S. actions.

To reduce the complexity of this topic, we offer a topology of fear that places each topical issue into a greater historical context, as illustrated in the following figure.

Although it oversimplifies the issues, this figure illustrates what is essentially a continuous process of fear utilization. When there is economic decline, fear becomes a catalyst for economic growth. In the context of a fear-driven economic cycle, one can argue

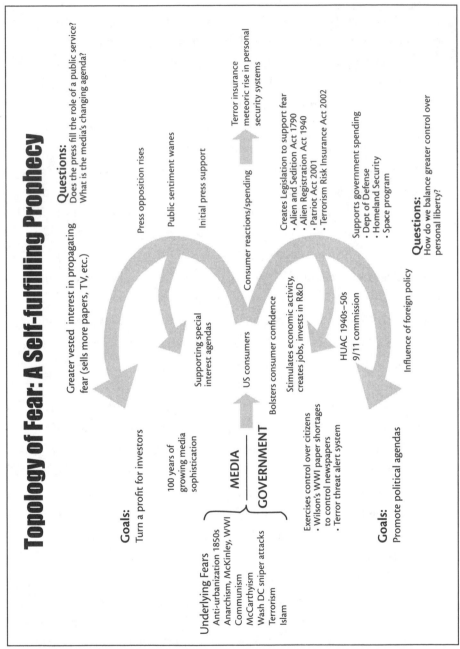

Figure 1. Topology of Fear: A Self-Fulfilling Prophecy

that terrorism is simply the next step in a logical progression of cause-and-effect geopolitical actions. Terrorist-based global conflict emerges simply because waging war against the technologically superior forces of the U.S. is too expensive for nation-states and non-state actors representing special interest groups or others. Simply put, government, business, and media do not invent fear, but they do tap into a *tradition* of fear which is as inherent to American society as is its desire for freedom.

This book is divided into four parts: Part I (*The Road to Fear Is Paved with Good Intentions*) argues that fear is an underlying characteristic of the American culture that has always been present as a legitimized mechanism for government control and economic activity. It argues that 9/11 merely brought the fear to the surface. We show how this cataclysmic attack is historically similar to previous fear-creating events like McCarthyism, *Sputnik*, and the Cold War. In all these instances, the globally interconnected media community has played an important role in fueling the nation's fears by using information and news to boost ratings and revenues, regardless of the consequences.

Part II (*The U.S. Fear / Threat Reaction and Global Defense*) discusses the perpetual cycle of fear needed to keep the U.S. economic engine in a constant state of growth. Using a variety of primary sources, such as declassified National Security Council planning documents, congressional records, U.S. demographic data, global macroeconomic statistics, and public speeches—coupled with secondary sources, including social commentary, contemporary books, and Hollywood movies—we provide evidence of historical patterns that suggest the easiest way to get America out of an economic slump is to start a war or an armed conflict requiring U.S. intervention. The fear/threat cycle is examined as a continuous loop

[handwritten margin note: tradition of fear? Susan Faludi]

that requires a response to boost American morale, which in turn stimulates the next generation of global unrest.

Part III (*Internalizing Fear: Venturing Down a Slippery Slope*) explores the nature of national fear in the context of the U.S. culture, using three distinct lenses: from a viewpoint of the need for fear; the long-term implications of the fear/threat–based foreign and domestic policies on liberty, freedom, and justice; and, finally, an examination of the decay in the American social fabric from continued use of this method of economic growth. In this sense, terrorism and the methods of terrorist groups such as Al-Qaeda represent a new period of history that we are entering, one in which the structures of political and economic power are no longer dictated by monetary power.

Part IV (*Breaking the Cycle of Fear: Can America Rebound?*) suggests several approaches and scenarios in which America can break the cycle of fear-generated cause-and-effect policy making. Avoiding an apocalyptic view of the future (providing both British and American perspectives), we use historical precedents such as the economic/military rise and fall of the British Empire and other great nations to illustrate possible trends in the decline of the American Empire. The authors examine the use of patriotism as a catalyst for fear to promote political and military objectives.

How has the U.S. as a nation coped with the introduction of Muslim terrorism in its daily life? Increased security, new laws, and new foreign policies are all indications of a developing new U.S. State, one where freedom is being continually reduced by fear. What are the other aspects of fear that are being introduced and developed into efficient discourses by U.S. politicians, economists, sociologists, and by the press? And how did the relationship between America as a free nation and fear begin? We intend to answer these and other important questions in the pages ahead.

Part I:
The Road to Fear Is Paved with Good Intentions

Fear makes the wolf bigger than he is.
—*German proverb*

ONE COULD ARGUE THAT ON 9/11, THE PEOPLE OF THE UNITED States lost the war on terror when fear of terrorism in all its forms replaced the proverbial American optimism. This statement, although shocking, rings true when viewed from the perspective of how effective terrorist actions have been in altering the American psyche. If indeed the objective of terrorism is to alter the behaviors and lifestyles of those who are its victims and to reduce them to a state of sustained fear, then it can be surmised that terrorism in America has prevailed. Reduced business travel, canceled vacations abroad, regular warnings on the news from the newly formed Department of Homeland Security of pending hostilities toward Americans, and other methods meant to "inform" us are a continual reminder that we need to fear our enemies, both foreign and domestic.

One question does arise: As the media and the government raced to design mechanisms to inform U.S. citizens of their vulnerability to attack, did they inadvertently play into the designs of the terrorists by placing the American people into a continual state of fear? The merchants of fear (government, media, business, and the terrorists) can only be effective if they have willing and eager customers who *want* to be afraid. What our research has shown is that U.S. citizens need to be afraid in order to be motivated. For example, polluting the environment is simply irresponsible; special interest groups have been advocating cleaning up the globe for the last four decades, while the average American has been little more than a spectator. But along came Al Gore recently anointed with a Nobel prize and his "end of the world as we know it" film, *An Inconvenient Truth,* complete with its own supporting new science of statistical elucidation, and suddenly, everyone is jumping on the "Green Bandwagon." We want to believe because we are afraid *not* to believe. The big question is, to what degree has fear altered America's understanding of itself? Is terrorism a greater threat than global warming?

One can argue that fear is relative, a fundamental human condition that is difficult to define because it is comprised of irrational dreads, superstitions, mythologies, beliefs, and perceptions. Fear is ubiquitous, existing within every level of society regardless of social class. Fears are both real and imagined, actual and predicted (for example, present in elderly people who fear crime or violence and rarely leave their homes, and also present in sudden sell-offs in the stock market for no rational or apparent reason).[5] Fears both real and imagined shape individual behaviors, thus determining how society reacts to domestic and foreign conditions. The relativity of fear spans a wide range of emotional states: anxiety, phobia, insecurity, uncertainty, threat, hatred, loathing, and trauma. What is important to remember is that fear on a societal level must be dealt with rationally, without pandering to the populism of an imagined state of fear.

When confronted with this idea—that fear is altering their behavior—Americans immediately move into a state of denial. Denying fear is an essential part of the government discourse that aims to rally patriotism and a sense of moral purpose in ridding the world of evil. The Aristotelian view of fear was that for governments, it provided a useful weapon to enforce moral and social order. However, a growing body of evidence suggests that the aura of fear is indeed present in the U.S.; even if it's not verbalized, it is certainly demonstrated by the actions of Americans. For example, the purchase of insurance policies against terrorist attacks shows that an economic consequence of fear is also very important. On November 26, 2002, the Terrorism Risk Insurance Act (TRIA) was signed into a law, intending to limit immediate market disruptions, encourage economic stabilization, and facilitate the transition to a private market for terrorism insurance.[6] In short, the birth of a new industry that caters exclusively to fear demonstrates America's new state of mind. The government's role is clear: It defined fear (The Patriot Act), and then established the rules whereby fear could be exploited (Terrorism Risk Insurance Act). Businesses now manufacture and sell products as antidotes for fear and as a warranty for peace of mind.

Here begins our discussion of the root causes of violent acts against Americans, the activities encased within U.S. foreign policy that act as a catalyst to ignite conflict, and the role of the media in perpetuating these affairs. Finally, we'll put forth a scenario based on American history as a means to speculate on possible long-term effects of the fear of terrorism in American society, economy, and culture. America's long association with fear as a motivating factor was noted in 1957 by General Douglas MacArthur:

Our government has kept us in a perpetual state of fear—kept us in a continuous stampede of patriotic fervor—with the cry of grave national emergency. Always there has been some terrible evil . . . to gobble us up if we did not blindly rally behind it by furnishing the exorbitant funds demanded. Yet, in retrospect, these disasters seem never to have happened, seem never to have been quite real.[7]

The next chapter discusses and highlights how the road to fear is paved with the special interest of U.S. businesses, such as the oil industry, which act as a counterproductive catalyst to thwart long-term global peace.

ONE

A History of Actions and Consequences

"We've been here before, Sam . . ."
—*J. R. R. Tolkien,* The Lord of the Rings

HENRY FORD, FAMED FOR HIS CLAIM THAT "HISTORY IS BUNK," may have known how to make automobiles—but he was no historian. History teaches us an invaluable lesson: that we have *always* been here before.

Consider the passing of the 2001 Patriot Act. This contentious piece of legislation, which we will examine in more detail later, is no more than a repetition of a similar attempt to frighten the American people back in the infancy of the Republic, in what Thomas Jefferson, who was horrified at such despotism, described as the "Republic of Witches." We see it, too, with even more eerie parallels to our own day, with Woodrow Wilson's attempt, shortly after America joined Britain and France against Germany in 1917, to suppress all possible dissent, and, for all intents and purposes, to abolish the constitutional rights of the American people to free speech.

In Britain, where citizens are subjects and where there is no written Constitution, one is well accustomed to the lack of freedom that Americans now suffer, post-9/11 and post–Patriot Act. One can only sympathize with the anger that many Americans feel at the threat to their liberty, not from foreign terrorism, but from the knee-jerk responses of the government in Washington, D.C. (and their parallels in London, to be fair). But we have survived such attempts to curtail our freedoms before, and, we trust, will do so again (particularly relevant for the winner of the 2008 U.S. presidential election, by the time you read this book).

Despite the intense anger that many Americans feel—a wrath that now encompasses not a few Republicans, as well as countless Democrats—the United States has survived attempts by totalitarian, dissent-hating, freedom-suppressing governments in Washington before. And, to be fair again to Republicans, the previous attempts were made not by dyed-in-the-wool Southern theocrats, but by the illustrious and otherwise highly laudable Federalists during the presidency of John Adams, and by that great idealist and apostle of self-determination, Woodrow Wilson, who, we should not forget, was the only Democratic president elected during the first three decades of the twentieth century.

No, like Tolkien's heroes Sam and Frodo, lost in the wilderness of Middle Earth, we have indeed been here before; the freedoms of the American people have not been irrevocably crushed, and democracy has not been extinguished. Those who have suppressed human rights and aimed to create a climate of fear, in the name of defeating foreign enemies, have not prevailed.

A Long History of Fear

Let us therefore look at two times where fear was the prime motivation for the suspension of liberties in order to pursue enemies of the state: first, when Americans feared French invasion in 1798;

and second, the fear of German espionage during what we now call World War I (then called the Great War), after the U.S. entered it in 1917. We will discover that however ill conceived the Patriot Act is, the lack of freedom of speech and exploitation of fear was in fact far worse during the past two instances than it is now.

In the same way that President George W. Bush supported the Patriot Act, in 1798, the U.S. Congress, led on by an equally controversial and potentially authoritarian president, John Adams, passed the Alien and Sedition Acts. Substitute France under Napoleon for Al-Qaeda terrorism, and it becomes apparent that there are many parallels between the events of 1798 and those of 2001. In each era of American history, we can view the actions of a president who wished to make illegal in varying degrees all opposition to his own regime. History, in other words, may repeat itself, but it is certainly not bunk, as it teaches us vital lessons for our own time.

The background to the legislation in the infant United States during the early days of the republic is twofold: First, in Europe, a continual state of hostility, sometimes including actual warfare, existed between Britain and France. Like America, the French had also recently experienced a revolution, although, in their case, it was considerably more violent, and led not to democracy but to dictatorship, with a young Corsican, Napoleon Bonaparte, seizing the effective reins of power. Many in the U.S. had been grateful to the old French monarchical regime for sending General Lafayette and effective military support to aid American forces in their struggle for independence. Britain, to them, remained an unfriendly power, especially to men such as Thomas Jefferson, who had lost both property and slaves at the hands of British troops. In Jefferson's case, he had also served as American ambassador to Paris, albeit mainly under the *ancien regime*.

Others took what would now be called a more "realist" attitude. Britain remained the world's predominant power, and French intentions, under the new regime of the directorate (the name given to the ruling body of revolutionaries) were far from certain.

Second, a difference arose among the founders of the new nation, regarding where the balance of power should lie. Some, like the first president, George Washington himself, and his secretary of the treasury, Alexander Hamilton, thought that the *predominant* power should lie at the center, with the federal government. They were therefore known as *Federalists*. John Adams, Washington's vice president, was also a Federalist, as was a promising young Virginia lawyer, John Marshall, a future chief justice of the United States.

On the other side stood Thomas Jefferson, Washington's inaugural secretary of state. With him were many Virginians, notably a future president, James Madison. They disliked too much power going to the center, and favored the rights of states, over and above that of the federal government. They feared that the centralizing tendencies of the Federalists would create an authoritarian state, and maybe even substitute monarchy for a republican form of government. Thus, they called themselves the Democratic-Republicans, or usually just *Republicans* for short.

When the war between the British and French became serious, George Washington, now the first president of the United States, declared his new nation strictly neutral. However grateful he may have been to the French, Britain was still too major a global power for the infant republic to antagonize. Then, in 1794, an American delegation to Britain negotiated a trade treaty with the British Empire, called the Jay Treaty. Supporters of France, like Thomas Jefferson, felt that this treaty jeopardized the United States and opened up the possibility of war with France. Other leaders, however, such as Alexander Hamilton, thought that good links with Britain made enormous economic sense for America, and strongly supported a policy of being robust toward the new French regime.

To Jefferson and others, all this was part and parcel of Hamilton and the Federalists' policy of *centripetalism*—bringing ever more power to the center. So when Washington decided not to stand again in 1796, John Adams stood as the candidate for the Federalists, and Jefferson for the Republicans. Owing to the vagaries of the then-new electoral college system, the winner of the election became president, and the candidate with the next-highest number of votes became vice president. John Adams narrowly won over Jefferson, so they became president and vice president respectively. Needless to say, this did not work, any more than a strongly ideological Democratic president and Republican vice president would work today.

But an already-tricky position was made far worse by the results of an American delegation to France in the spring of 1798, with John Marshall being one of the three key delegates. The mission not only failed, but it did so with a strong whiff of corruption on the French side. Three key interlocutors, known only as X, Y, and Z, were found to have requested a substantial bribe to press the American suit upon the French directorate. This was refused, and two of the American delegates, including Marshall, stormed back to the United States. Public opinion now swung zealously behind that of the Federalist president, Adams, and his cause. Marshall, already a revered commander from the Revolutionary War, returned home to a lyrical hero's welcome, and also to the plaudits of his great mentor, Washington himself. The French, as in 2003 with the introduction of "freedom fries" to replace french fries, were widely seen as the enemy, and as an object of scorn. War between the U.S. and France was now a distinct possibility.

Had matters stopped there, it would not have been so worrying—although it did put natural Francophiles, such as Thomas Jefferson, in an awkward position. But unfortunately, as in 2001, the president and his administration, with overwhelming congressional support, decided to make major political capital out of the threat of war and of the surge in patriotism expressed by the American people.

Four acts, all passed overwhelmingly by a majority Federalist Congress, came onto the statute book in swift succession, each duly signed into law by the president. The first was the Naturalization Act, which extended the amount of time a new citizen had to have lived in America, from five years to fourteen. Professor James Simon has called this a partisan act, since the majority of those whose citizenship was now delayed, mainly immigrants from France and Ireland, were known to be supporters of Jefferson's Republicans.

Second was the Alien Enemies Act, which gave the president the right to confine or expel enemy aliens during war; here, it seems, even a few Republicans voted for the measure.

Third was the Alien Act. This enabled the president to summarily expel any aliens found guilty of being simply dangerous to the "peace and safety" of the United States. Here due process of law was abolished—the expulsions could be made without any recourse to jury trial. Nor would the president be required to explain his decision. Not surprisingly, Jefferson scornfully considered the Alien Act "worthy of the eighth or ninth century."

Finally, there was the most totalitarian of all four acts—the Sedition Act. This legislation also overrode the new Bill of Rights, in that it completely negated the Bill's guarantee of freedom of speech. The act provided for a $2,000 fine and up to two years in prison for "false, scandalous and malicious" accusations against the president, Congress, or the government.

Significantly, as James Simon has noted, Jefferson, the vice president, was not so protected. Not surprisingly, Jefferson wrote that summer to his friend, James Madison, about the Federalists, noting:

> *They have brought into the lower house a sedition bill which, among other enormities, undertakes to make printing certain matters criminal, though one of the amendments to the Constitution [the Bill of Rights] has so expressly taken . . . printing presses . . . out of their coercion. Indeed, this bill and the alien bill both are so palpably in the teeth of the Constitution as to show they mean to pay no respect to it.*

Not even democratically elected congressmen were immune. One of the first successful prosecutions and imprisonments was that of congressman Matthew Lyon, whose opposition to the political position of the Federalists landed him in jail. To Jefferson and others, this was the beginning of totalitarianism. This was, Jefferson wrote, the "reign of witches."

One of the most controversial phrases of the Sedition Act was the second clause, which stated:

> *That if any person shall write, print, utter, or publish, or shall cause or procure to be written, printed, uttered, or published, or shall knowingly and willingly assist or aid in writing, printing, uttering, or publishing any false, scandalous, and malicious writing or writings against the Government*

of the United States, or either house of the Congress . . . or the President . . . or to bring any of them, or either of them, into contempt or disrepute; or to excite against them . . . the hatred of the good people of the United States, or to stir up sedition within the United States, or to excite any unlawful combination therein, for opposing or resisting any law of the United States, or any act of the President of the United States. . . .

Thus, the basic premise of the Sedition Act is to define opposition in the broadest possible terms so it can be applied to as many circumstances as possible, just as the definition of terrorism in the twenty-first century Patriot Act enables us to classify almost anyone as a terrorist.

Under the Sedition Act, people engaged in dissent or public opposition would face the jail sentence mentioned earlier. This was entirely against the provisions of the Constitution in favor of freedom of speech. It was also entirely political in scope; editors who were sympathetic to Jefferson were jailed, rather than seditious French agents, against whom the act was theoretically aimed.

Not surprisingly perhaps, on July 5, 2004, *Time* magazine accurately described the Sedition Act as the "Patriot Act of the 18th Century," for, then as now, "it was common practice to question the patriotism of citizens, immigrants and the political opposition." Yet today we have forgotten the words of Samuel Johnson on April 7, 1775 reminding us that "patriotism is the last refuge of a scoundrel", referring to the use of patriotism as a pretext to advance hidden political agendas. Fortunately for Jefferson, many of the state politicians in Virginia and Kentucky realized, as he did, that the acts were a major threat to the constitutional liberties of the newly free

American people. Jefferson himself secretly drafted the Kentucky resolution against the acts, and Madison performed a similar function in Virginia. They realized that the recent Tenth Amendment to the Constitution stated that local states could reserve to themselves powers not specifically granted to the federal government by the Constitution, and that Kentucky and Virginia could thereby prevent the operation of the acts within their own territories.

The Virginia Resolution of 1798 declared that the acts would "transform the present republican system of the United States, into an absolute, or at best mixed monarchy." The acts subverted the Constitution itself, and the right to free speech in particular.

The Kentucky Resolution of 1799 was even more robust, reflecting Jefferson's utter disgust at the totalitarian tendencies of the Adams legislation. Adams was trying to impose the "fangs of despotism" on "the good people of this commonwealth," and any form of "silent acquiescence" of such legislation would be "highly criminal."

As Jefferson wrote despairingly to a friend about the Acts, "For my own part, I consider those laws as . . . an experiment on the American mind, to see how far it will bear an avowed violation of the Constitution. If this goes down, we shall immediately see attempted another act of Congress declaring that the President shall continue in office during life"—and, Jefferson worried, the Senate the same, also for life.

Jefferson was surely being unfair to Adams, who never contemplated a lifelong presidency. But as Jefferson and others did not hesitate to point out, freedom of speech was a vital component of any true democracy, and to restrict it in so blatantly partisan a way was bound to seriously harm the cause of freedom and of democratic accountability.

Thankfully, for that cause, Jefferson won the presidency in 1800, albeit only by a slight margin, and after much deliberation. The contentious acts expired, although their ghosts lingered on until 1964, when, in *The New York Times vs. Sullivan*, they were finally expunged.

Countless Parallels

The parallels between 1798 and the early twenty-first century are, alas, all too many. The 2001 Patriot Act was passed in a similar war panic, and with equally unfortunate results for civil liberties, which we will examine in more detail. Even France appears twice, as the enemy in 1798, and the country that refused to aid the U.S. in 2003. People opposed to the government have been as personally vilified now as then, labeled unpatriotic, immoral, or anti-Christian. (Nothing changes . . .) Several cities have passed resolutions against the Patriot Act, as Kentucky and Virginia did in the 1790s.

But perhaps the most noticeable overlap is in terms of freedom of the individual and freedom of speech. If one searches for references to the Patriot Act on Google, for example, many of them are from angry librarians. This is because, as *Slate* notes, Section 215 of the Act in effect "authorizes the Government to march into a library and demand a list of everyone who's ever checked out a copy of *The Secret Garden*."

Section 215 explains that the director of the FBI, or any suitable FBI employee, "may make an application for an order requiring the production of any tangible things (including books, records, papers, documents, and other items) for an investigation to protect against international terrorism or clandestine intelligence activities, provided that such investigation of a United States person is not conducted solely on the basis of activities protected by the first amendment to the Constitution."

As *Slate* puts it, "Post–Patriot Act, third-party holders of your financial, library, travel, video rental, phone, medical, church, synagogue, and mosque records can be searched without your knowledge or consent, providing the government says it's protecting against terrorism."

Under Section 218, Americans are not exempt from the Foreign Intelligence Surveillance Act applying to them, which means you can be bugged without your knowledge. Sections 411 and 412 of the act mirror almost exactly the provisions of the 1798 acts that authorized aliens to be removed from the country, even if you did not know you were helping a terrorist, but "reasonably should have known" that you were.

Clearly, in each historical period, these restrictive acts were both inspired and, their proponents would all argue, justified by the reigning climate of fear. As we will show with numerous examples throughout this book, the exploitation of fear after 9/11 is not a new phenomenon in American history. The use of fear to justify political actions—including the inhibition of private actions and personal expression—goes back in kind to the infancy of the Republic.

The deliberate stirring up and misuse of fear is as old as the United States (and in other countries, like the United Kingdom, obviously older still). In the coming chapters we shall look at many more instances, including the fear of Catholicism in the nineteenth century and the Espionage Act of 1917, which made opposition to the Wilson administration's decision to enter World War I a criminal offense.

Ten Years in Jail for Michael Moore . . .

Imagine if Michael Moore had not garnered film awards for *Fahrenheit 911* or *Bowling for Columbine*, but a ten-year jail sentence instead. No doubt many avid Republicans would have no objections to Moore's films being absent from the screen for quite some time, but it would be an exceptionally hardened few who would actually want him to face jail, let alone a sentence as long as ten years. But the equivalent has happened, and under a *Democratic* president, Woodrow Wilson.

This was the fate of Robert Goldstein, the producer of the 1917 silent film, *The Spirit of '76*. While the Eugene Debs case (which we will soon discuss) is well known, perhaps reflecting the liberal bias of textbook writers, the trial and conviction of Goldstein is less infamous. This is a shame, because while it could be said that Debs actively courted martyrdom—albeit in the truly noble cause of free speech—it almost certainly never occurred to poor Goldstein that he was doing anything remotely wrong, let alone committing a federal offense that was to land him a totally disproportionate and draconian ten-year sentence.[8]

Goldstein, Thomas Fleming reminds us, served as an assistant to the legendary D. W. Griffith on the latter's epic movie, *Birth of a Nation*. It seemed a good idea to Goldstein to follow this up with a film that portrayed the way in which the infant Republic gained its independence from Britain, so he conceived and produced *The Spirit of '76*. This naturally involved portraying British soldiers (including the Hessian mercenaries, who were in fact German) as deeply unsympathetic, and, in some cases, guilty of committing atrocities against the brave rebel population. Historically, while the amount of massacres has perhaps been exaggerated in the patriotic imagination, there is no doubt at all that some did occur, and so Goldstein was only portraying what had actually happened.

But the law was of wide remit; anything that criticized Wilson's war policy—or, as Goldstein discovered, the acts over a century before of one of America's allies, Great Britain—was now thoroughly illegal. Showing British soldiers murdering brave Americans, even though it took place over 140 years ago, was showing an ally in a bad light, and thus, perceived as possibly providing help to the German enemy. The judge, according to Fleming, accused Goldstein of "exaggerated scenes of British cruelty" that would cause moviegoers to "question the good faith of our ally, Great Britain." In particular, soldiers seeing the film might be vulnerable. So Goldstein was sentenced to ten years in a federal penitentiary.

What had he done that was so heinous?

The answer is that he had broken the law as dictated by the 1917 Espionage Act, a piece of legislation that has rightly been called the worst since the 1798 equivalents, because, as interpreted, they were in fact far more about the oppression and suppression of domestic *political* opponents than of foreign spies, of whom there were, in fact, hardly any at all. The Espionage Act—along with its 1918 strengthening piece of legislation, the Sedition Act—made unlawful any criticism of the conduct of the war, since anyone who claimed that the administration made any mistakes at all was seen as being on the side of the enemy, Germany.

The Resurrection of Old Fears

Now this concept—those who are not actively with us are against us—is a familiar one, as President George W. Bush has resurrected it unashamedly since 9/11, to deem even the faintest whiff of criticism of administration incompetence as tantamount to a public declaration of support for Osama bin Laden, Al-Qaeda, and terrorist attacks against the U.S. This notion is as nonsensical today (and, more pertinently, perhaps, since 2003) as it was in 1917–1918.

However, one can also say that whatever the failings of the Bush administration, countless books—including plenty of good ones, such as the award-winning *Imperial Life in the Emerald City: Inside Iraq's Green Zone*—have been freely published without any prosecution against their authors by the Bush regime. Rajiv Chandrasekaran, the author of *Imperial Life*, was not jailed, let alone prosecuted, and even those whose works are sometimes on shakier factual ground, such as those of the infamous Michael Moore himself, remain free and at liberty.

In other words, while it is certainly true, as many journalists have now openly admitted, that the press was far too craven and fearful as a result of 9/11 in exposing the initial phases of the war in Iraq, nothing today, even the worst excesses of the Patriot Act, are even remotely commensurate with the highly oppressive, censoring, and quasidictatorial regime of Woodrow Wilson in 1917–1919, amid the effects of the Espionage Act of 1917 and its sequel, the Sedition Act of 1918.

To put it another way, if all this seems very familiar, anything said in the twenty-first century about George W. Bush and his overwhelming sense of divine mission and self-righteousness can be applied in considerably parallel detail to the wartime conduct of Woodrow Wilson, or, to use a hideous but descriptive piece of political science jargon, the two *idealist* presidents in foreign policy of the last hundred years. Yes, Wilson was a Democrat, but, also yes, we have very much been here before, in that his idealism in its domestic effects has had the same oppressive outcome as that of his Republican but equally idealist successor, George W. Bush. Their political parties might be different, but their idealism and the concomitant use of domestic fear is identical.

Academic freedom in the U.S. was also threatened as a result of 9/11. On November 11, 2001, the American Council of Trustees and Alumni released a report including the names of academics who had made public statements and/or questioned the government's actions in the war against terrorism.[9] But one does not have to be an academic to be under surveillance in America. Since 9/11, the government has encouraged the creation of citizen-sentinels who promote a "national neighborhood watch" whereby all individuals aim to be vigilant and to spy on their fellow countrymen and -women to ensure that they are not promoting terror. This is indeed the way in which the USSR was depicted in the 1960s, when some of us grew up—as a society of spies.

Vigilance, of course, is not restricted to the government watching academics and individuals watching individuals. American citizens who read a politically liberal newspaper or journal at their local public library, under the Patriot Act, will be recorded. (It is best not to think of what can happen if someone borrows a book sympathetic to, say, extremist Islam. . . .) However, the fact is that such newspapers still exist, their opposition to George W. Bush notwithstanding. Surveillance does not mean the closing down of these newspapers and shutting up the opposition. This was not the case under the Espionage and Sedition Acts, when the postmaster general, Albert Burleson, was able to use the powers conferred upon him in those acts to close down any newspaper or journal that contained "false reports or false statements with the intent to interfere with the operation or success of the military. . . ."

This interference was interpreted very broadly indeed, and, as Wilson wrote to *The New York Times*, this draconian breadth of censorship was "absolutely necessary to the public safety." Furthermore, as the Espionage Act decreed, a breach of this law would involve a $10,000 fine (in 1917 values) or twenty years in jail.

As Eric Foner puts it in his helpful book, *Give Me Liberty! An American History*:

> *World War I raised questions . . . glimpsed during the Civil War that would trouble the nation again during the McCarthy era and the aftermath of the terrorist attacks of 2001: What is the balance between security and freedom? Does the Constitution protect citizens' rights during wartime? Should dissent be equated with lack of patriotism?*

The parallels are strong, despite the fact that Wilson and Bush Jr. are best described as being at opposite ends of the political spectrum on *domestic* politics. Nonetheless, one could argue that both of them were *idealists* in foreign policy, wishing to impose what they felt beyond argument to be right upon the peoples of the world. In Wilson's case, the great tragedy was the failure of the U.S. to remain part of the global system after 1921, and to retreat into isolationism. Thus, America was not in a position to stop Hitler in the 1930s, a mistake very carefully avoided by Truman after 1945, and, in his case, with the full consent of the Congress and the overwhelming majority of Americans, Republicans and Democrats alike. This was also a consensus which endured until the 1990s, as Georgetown University professor Charles Kupchan has eloquently argued in the magazine, *Foreign Affairs*. George W. Bush's failings are, in some ways, too recent to write about objectively, but the fact that many Republicans are now rejecting his unfortunate legacy in Iraq shows that he too might leave a legacy of disaster behind him.

We now return to the days of 1917, although many other parallels between then and now will inevitably emerge. Serious money and a national campaign also helped to ensure there were no slackers in terms of supporting the war, and, to guarantee that there would be enough soldiers to fight it, a then-rare peacetime draft. In charge of propaganda was the Karl Rove of his day, George Creel, a journalist originally from Missouri who, it seems, described himself as a solid "Woodrow Wilson man." He gained massive funding for his Committee on Public Information, which was, as all these things inevitably prove to be, often perceived as a cheerleading enterprise for the administration.

In addition to making certain that the press had the best spin—*spin doctor* or spinmeister might be a new term, but the concept is a very old one—he also established a group of what he called "Four Minute Men," a historic term, but with a new purpose: to get out and about in towns across America and spread the good news of the administration's goals and its defense of freedom. Creel soon enlisted over 75,000 such Four Minute speakers, to preach the cause across the land.

But local people soon co-opted themselves in what Richard Gamble has justly described as the *War for Righteousness* (also the title of his book). Gamble gives due prominence to the many popularly created leagues or associations, the most eminent and effective of which was the American Protective League, which very soon had over a quarter of a million patriotic Americans at its beck and call. The APL has become infamous, especially on the political Left. There is a good reason for this.

As Barbara Tuchman reminds us in her legendary book on the origins of World War I, *The Guns of August*, the start of hostilities split the hitherto united European political Left. In Britain, the

Labor Party itself was of two minds, some supporting and others opposing, on the grounds that they could not sustain what many of them regarded as a capitalist war. However, as Tuchman (and, in more academic works, Isaiah Berlin) demonstrate, European socialists tended to vote not as one solid Europe-wide unified socialist bloc, but instead as patriots, with the French socialists supporting the war against the national enemy (Germany), and the German socialists similarly voting to support their emperor, Kaiser Wilhelm II, against democratic France and Britain.

In the U.S., the socialists, under their leader, Eugene Debs, took the same view as the Labor Party minority in Britain; namely, that as this was a war between capitalist powers, they as socialists should have nothing to do with it.

Up until 1917 this was no problem; after all, Wilson won his reelection campaign in 1916 with the slogan that he would keep the U.S. out of what many regarded (then as now) as a matter purely of European concern. Then, in 1917, two crucial events took place. One, obviously, was that Wilson changed and the U.S. entered the war after all, on the side of the democracies against the imperialist regimes of Germany, Austria-Hungary, and the Ottoman Empire. This in itself put the socialists in a bind.

But then, worse still for them, Russia left the war. Up until the first of the two Russian revolutions that year, imperial Russia's place on the Allied side was always somewhat of an embarrassment, since a regime that had not hesitated to shoot its workers could hardly be described as a democracy. The first revolution—about which we often forget—solved this problem, since it was clearly pro-democracy and, what is more, wanted to continue on the Allied side. But, despite its best efforts, and that of its most eminent leader, Kerensky, it became even more bogged in the mire than before, and in the October Revolution (in *November* 1917), this moderate regime was overthrown by Lenin and his Bolsheviks.

We forget today how terrified people were of this new Bolshevik specter, which, as the Bolsheviks were proud to point out, was soon haunting not just Europe, but the rest of the world, through institutions such as the International Workers of the World, or "Wobblies." The fact that in the twenty-first century a large socialist movement is all but inconceivable in the U.S. is proof of the savagery with which they were suppressed in 1917, and afterward.

One of the first things that Lenin did was to decide to concentrate on consolidating the revolution within Russia itself. This entailed withdrawing from the war, which was something the Germans hoped he would do in any case, since both he and his Bolshevik followers had promised this as part of their manifesto. German faith in Lenin was not misplaced; in 1918, the new Bolshevik government signed the Treaty of Brest-Litovsk, and the infant Soviet state withdrew from the war.

This meant that in the eyes of many patriotic Americans, all socialists were traitors, friends of the national enemy, Germany. The fact that domestic socialists such as Debs had so vigorously opposed entry to the war only confirmed this bad impression. So now, by definition, to be a socialist was to be anti-American—a traitor—and soon, International Workers of the World offices were trashed by angry mobs who were, as often as not, then found not guilty of any crime.

Many socialist newspapers had been closed down because they opposed the draft—an act of repression that did not happen again during similar periods of national dissent, such as over Vietnam or, more recently, over Iraq (when there was no draft as such, but many unsuspecting National Guardsmen suddenly found themselves on front-line duty in war-torn parts of downtown Baghdad).

Debs, one could argue, almost sought martyrdom, as he went out of his way to be provocative. The Sedition Act of 1918 was even more catch-all and repressive than the Espionage Act of the year before, since it outlawed anything that might throw "contempt, scorn, or disrepute" on what it described as the "form of government." Over a thousand people were convicted on this very wide interpretation of dissent, and Debs was by far the most famous. In 1918 he was convicted of making an antiwar speech, and, like Goldstein, was sentenced to ten years in prison. His speech in defense of freedom was to become legitimately famous, containing principles that hopefully all of us could agree with, even those of us who might disagree with socialism as a political doctrine. As he put it in his words to the jury before being sent down:

> In every age there have been a few heroic souls who have been in advance of their time, who have been misunderstood, maligned, persecuted, sometimes even put to death ... Washington, Jefferson, Franklin, Paine ... were the rebels of their day ... But they had the moral conviction to be true to their convictions. . . . [The] leaders of the abolition movement ... were regarded as public enemies and treated accordingly, were true to their convictions and stood their ground ... [America had been in controversial wars before, but those who opposed them] were not indicted; they were not charged with treason ... I believe in the right of free speech, in war as well as in peace.

As the great commentator Walter Lippman once put it, the repression of civil liberties during this period showed, alas, "that the traditional liberties of speech and opinion rest on no solid foundation."

The parallels between then and now continue. Not only did the APL try to root out all popular dissent—John White, a farmer from Iowa, received a twenty-one-month prison sentence for no more than a few words in an unguarded conversation, when he suggested that German atrocities in Belgium were no worse than those committed by American troops in the Philippines after 1899—but also, just as "French fries" became "Freedom Fries" after 2003 (when France made the decision not to back the invasion of Iraq), the innocent hamburger became a "liberty sandwich" and sauerkraut was transformed into "liberty cabbage." In the same way that a poor Sikh was murdered after 9/11 by someone who mistook him for a Muslim (as if killing a Muslim would have been acceptable), the Swiss conductor of the Boston Symphony Orchestra was interned as an enemy alien for the heinous crime of playing Beethoven (who was, in fact, an Austrian).

The final nail in the coffin was the notorious "clear and present danger" interpretation of the Supreme Court in 1919, which legitimized repression of the First Amendment of freedom of speech if times of conflict overrode the right to speak freely. This was the Charles Schenck case, and the main judgment that contained the now-famous phrase was that of Justice Oliver Wendell Holmes. Charles Schenck, like Debs, was a socialist, and in his case, he had been posting antidraft leaflets through the mail, an act that was, the Supreme Court ruled, illegal. Holmes argued that it was the equivalent of a man in a theater "falsely shouting 'Fire!' . . . and causing a panic."

Holmes has always been considered one of the most eminent liberal judges on the Supreme Court, but this judgment was anything but liberal. Government, and now the judiciary, were both backing illiberal repression of what one could argue was *domestic* dissent in time of war overseas. Whatever one might think of Schenck's politics, or of his opposition to American involvement on the side of the democracies against German imperialism, he certainly did not deserve a stretch in prison for what was a purely political opposition to a foreign war. Fear of German spies, fear of what legitimate dissent would do to the war effort—these created an atmosphere of narrow-minded oppression that did America's great tradition of freedom of speech no good at all.

McCarthy and Beyond...

If Hitler said that two and two made four, does that mean that we, as believers in liberal democracy, freedom, justice, and the rule of law, ought now to argue that, in fact, they make five? Obviously the answer to that is no! Some things are true regardless of who says them.

The same is true with many of the issues dating from the early 1950s and the McCarthy era, as those now deeply regretted few years show us. Strictly speaking, this was an era—as described by David Caute in his book, *The Great Fear*—in which an opposition senator created the climate of fear rather than the government itself, as in 1798 and 1917. Nonetheless, the whole atmosphere of the country was so altered by it that we need to consider it in detail, as much as the eras of the two Sedition Acts.

In recent years, thanks to various KGB defectors to the West (and to various intercepts Britain and the USA succeeded in making from Soviet communications traffic), we know that there really were large numbers of genuine communist spies working in the West during the McCarthy period. The Venona decrypts have proved that one of these spies was Alger Hiss, the top State Department official accused of being just that by Whittaker Chambers, Senator McCarthy, and the up-and-coming Republican politician,

Richard Nixon. Ironically, McCarthy never got the names of most of the *real* spies, nearly all of whom were not exposed until twenty, thirty, and even forty or more years later, in some cases long after their deaths. His infamous list of 205 communist agents whose names and identities were fully known to the secretary of state was pure gibberish, and, as we know, he was never able to prove any of it, since most of his accusations were figments of his over-heated and tortured imagination. So the fact that in both Britain and the U.S., there really were Soviet spies out there, about whom McCarthy had no knowledge, is rather ironic!

Some right-wing commentators have claimed what we now know to be the truth as a vindication of what McCarthy was up to during the peak of his 1950s infamy. McCarthy was obsessed with Hollywood, where there were no Soviet spies trying to turn patriotic Americans into Communists through the cinema, and where the vicious policy of "blacklisting" supposed subversives made not a whit of difference to American internal security. In fact, it resulted only in the destruction of some of the ablest talents the film industry has ever produced. McCarthy really was loathsome, and richly deserved his comeuppance when it finally came.

Where McCarthy is important is in connection with the main theme of our book: the creation of a climate of fear, and the use of that fear for blatant domestic political purposes, a point made very clear in, for example, the excellent book, *Give Me Liberty* by Eric Foner, and in older works such as Hugh Brogan's *The Penguin History of the USA* and in Samuel Eliot Morrison's classic, *The Oxford History of the American People*.

The *real* issue, one can argue, was not actually communist infiltration at all. The important fact was that Roosevelt had kept the Republicans out of the White House for sixteen years, and that Truman's unexpected win in 1948 meant that it would be two decades out of power for them by the time of the next presidential election in 1952. Although the Republicans briefly won the Congress in 1946, they were not able to keep hold of it, and this was denying more than one generation of Republican leaders the power to which they aspired.

Many of those accused of being Soviet spies were in fact loyal Roosevelt Democrats, architects of the New Deal—patriotic but politically liberal Americans who, to the increasing disgust of the excluded Republicans, kept on winning power.

Anti-communism, and the lack of patriotism that inevitably accompanied such charges, was therefore a boon to desperate Republicans, anxious to find any stick with which to beat their seemingly invincible domestic political enemies. In a very few cases, such as that of Alger Hiss, the accusations were actually true. But in the overwhelming majority of the claims, they were complete nonsense— vicious smears upon loyal Americans who dared to hold what was perceived by Republican Party stalwarts as the "wrong" views.

One of the recent best-sellers on how Americans vote is Thomas Frank's book, *What's The Matter With Kansas? How Conservatives Won the Heart of America*. Here the author shows that millions of Americans vote not according to their feelings on economic issues, but on hot-button cultural issues. Experts, such as University of Virginia sociologist James Davison Hunter, have called this phenomenon the *culture wars*, and it is probably fair to say that using cultural as opposed to economic arguments has helped the Republicans in their recent successful hold on power (albeit, less effective in the 2006 congressional elections, and with effects as yet unknown, at this writing, in the November 2008 presidential race). Issues such as gay marriage, writers have argued, motivate blue-collar Americans into voting Republican, even though that party benefits the rich rather than those with lower incomes.

While commentators would probably agree that the current culture wars do not go back further than the 1960s and the Nixon reaction to the excesses of the Flower Power era, one could argue that what made McCarthy so effective, especially in his attacks on the Hollywood elite, is in many ways a progenitor of later culture-war attacks on those seen by the blue-collar classes as un-American and unpatriotic. McCarthy's base was, after all, the House Committee on *Un-American* Activities.

Eisenhower, we know, was no fan of McCarthy, even though he did choose as his vice president one of that senator's few astute political allies, Richard Nixon, who was thus placed a heartbeat away from the presidency at the young age of thirty-nine. McCarthy was destroyed through his own corruption and cupidity—but then, he was no longer necessary, since there was now a Republican in the White House again, after twenty years of political exile. McCarthy was always crude and egotistical (his hallmarks, after all), but, one could say, he had done his job and could now be safely removed as the embarrassment he had long since become.

One should also remember that even Truman—not highly rated then, but now seen as one of America's greatest and most significant presidents—introduced, in the 1940s, an extra loyalty oath that had to be taken by all federal employees. This was constitutionally unnecessary, but was insisted upon all the same. This excluded not just obvious traitors but those of left-wing, heterodox opinions from even the lowliest of jobs and, almost certainly, made no difference whatsoever to the internal security of the early Cold War United States.

What the McCarthy era did, therefore, was to create a climate of internal fear, of "Reds under the beds," of unknown, malevolent forces, poisoning drinking water with chloride (to take as an example one prevalent but entirely bogus terror), of introducing communism and Soviet domination to freedom-loving, patriotic Americans. Not only that, but it also fulfilled a crucial goal: making most voters naturally think of the Republicans as the party of national security, the people who would make you safe against *Them*, the bad guys, the cowboys in the black hats, the communists, the Soviet threat, and nuclear annihilation.

And Further Beyond...

To some extent, one could add, this has remained the case for decades, even after the fall of the Soviet Union (and thus, of the Red Menace) in 1991. The 2004 election is surely proof positive of this contention—we will look at the subject of the war on terror in more detail elsewhere—in that the core issue was that under Bush, the Republicans would protect America from its foes in a way (they argued) that the Democrats simply could not.

(At the time of writing in mid-2007, it is too soon to tell whether the Iraq debacle will have long-term effects in removing this security advantage from the Republicans. It is certainly fascinating to watch how many in that party are trying to distance themselves from Bush's clear failure to achieve military victory in Iraq. It would certainly be ironic if one of the most right-wing Republican presidents in many a year ended up destroying a decades-old Republican advantage over the Democrats!)

So although McCarthy is long dead, the principle of what he was doing has a strong degree of historical continuity behind it, stretching back to 1798 and the attempt to demonize Jefferson and his supporters, as being pro-French, and of Woodrow Wilson to achieve the same goals, of accusing anyone who criticized his way of running the war as an enemy of the American people. From the Federalists, to Wilson, to McCarthy, and the Republican gibes of 2001 onward—namely, that those who are not with us are against us, and thus not true, patriotic Americans—the technique has remained exactly the same. Create fear, besmirch your internal political enemies as traitors, crush all political opposition (by draconian new laws, if possible), and hope that the votes come trickling in.

This is why history is important. There is a feeling among many Democrats that the era of George W. Bush is a uniquely awful aberration in the otherwise sane history of American politics. In fact, as we have seen, there have been eras of oppression and repression far *worse* than anything George W. may have committed. What has happened before can happen again, and very easily too. Vigilance is *always* essential, and we must remember that it was a Democratic president, Woodrow Wilson, under whom domestic critics were jailed for ten years and more. This was a president whom, as we have observed, proclaimed freedom, justice, and all the right idealist aims, and actually meant them, too. As the old saying goes, the road to hell is paved with good intentions. Wilson stands as living proof of how great ideals can go horribly wrong.

No, the truth is that politicians of *all* parties and persuasions have used, and continue to use, fear as a means of domestic control, the terror of the outside enemy to suppress dissent at home. Whether it was the French under Napoleon, Germany under the Kaiser, the Soviet Union with Reds under the beds, or Al-Qaeda in our own time, real threats overseas become means of suppression domestically. As another saying goes (in translation): The more things change, the more they stay the same.

[handwritten margin note: fear of outside enemy]

Were Colonial Americans a Vintage Version of Terrorists?

Placing the broad contemporary definition of terrorism as adopted by the U.S. Congress in the Patriot Act into a historical context, one could postulate that colonial America was founded by direct acts of anticolonial terrorism against the ruling British government. The early colonial "acts of terror" were designed to oust a distant ruling government in favor of local self-rule, and in effect move against a foreign power on domestic soil. In the modern context, terrorism associated with the political agendas of the Middle East can be interpreted as a series of deliberate acts against the invasion of a foreign culture on a domestic lifestyle, or the influence of Western lifestyles acting as "cultural terrorism," ultimately destabilizing local value systems. Americans have forgotten that the only democratically elected government in the Middle East was overthrown by the U.S. when it orchestrated the 1953 coup to oust the government of Mohammed Mossedegh (modern day Iran) after he nationalized the oil industry in 1951. Therefore, placing the definition of terrorism within a broader historical context, one could put forward the idea that terrorism is relative to who is the recipient or originator; one man's terrorist is another man's freedom fighter. Hence, the eradication of terrorism needs to address not only the underlying root cause, but must also set in motion a mechanism to ensure that the nations of the world work in concert to achieve a mutually beneficial agenda, such as a stable economy, and security and civil rights for all.

However, the greater threat to freedom is not a breach of security by foreign enemies, but rather from within the nation itself, as a by-product of terrorism—and that is, put simply, domestic fear. Manifesting itself as legislation driven by emotions, fear, and racial prejudice, the goal of terrorism is made complete by the passage of seemingly defensive new laws, enacted after September 11th. Once again we fail to see the foresight of America's founding fathers in a modern context as U.S. president James Madison, at the Virginia Convention of 1788, warns us of the vigilance we must have in safeguarding freedom:

Since the general civilisation of mankind, I believe there are more instances of the abridgement of freedom of the people, by gradual and silent encroachments of those in power, than by violent and sudden usurpations.[10]

The American culture has a history of being driven by fear as a primary motivator of Richard M. Nixon's often-silent majority. This conditioned fear can quite possibly be traced back to the nation's Anglo-Protestant roots as a God-fearing people, which was a popular doctrine in the past. Fear is used to generate political homogeneity within a community or nation by creating fear of the "other."[11] To do this, any moral discourse must be dissipated typically by character assassination or simply by dismissing them as unpatriotic. Fear is used politically to create a sense of besiegement by "the others," such as linking corporate outsourcing to foreign countries with domestic job losses. Fear plays on the lack of reasoned argument within oneself. For example, in the case of outsourcing, numerous research projects have demonstrated that job loss to foreign outsourcing is only a relatively small contributor to declining jobs, at just 2.4 percent.[12] However, politicians, trade unions, and the media continuously use this fear in their rhetoric when trying to promote their agendas.

Another form of besiegement is the sense of cultural dissipation, or the loss of traditional values because of the actions of a specific group or technology. In the cold light of reality, fear is often used as a deterrent to keep the actions of people within the boundaries of accepted social behavior. However, one could argue that criminals ignore the fear/threat consequences, and fear as a deterrent is primarily used to keep law-abiding citizens in check. Thus the old adage, locks are meant to keep honest people honest because a determined criminal will always get in or out. A lack of recognition of actions/consequences may account for why military reprisals have been an ineffective deterrent of terrorism because they are designed for nation-states who recognize the consequences of an action. Terrorist groups who are non-state actors operate independent of national boundaries, irrespective of the consequence of their actions, thereby minimizing the effectivity of large-scale military actions. Thus terrorists do not have the same fear of reprisal that is shared by state actors such as a politician's fear of not being re-elected.

Past fear-based movements, such as the Salem witch trials and the anti-urbanization movement of the 1840s, are examples of times when government and/or society in general used fear to ignite social change. This was done by raising the citizenry's consciousness to a perceived threat as a prelude to building a case for the employment of a moral high ground to promote specific goals and objectives. A good example of this concept is the fear of urbanism, when rising city populations were viewed as a threat to morality; middle-class women were seen as especially vulnerable to sexual dangers of urban space. Cities introduced regulations on women traveling within cities to make them feel safer, which, on the contrary, increased their anxiety.[13]

We must avoid being driven by fear and strive to look beyond the immediate pain and sorrow in order to address the fundamental preservation of freedom and the reestablishment of domestic security. We must ask ourselves: What kind of tradeoffs are we making between security and freedom?

American culture has historically used—and continues to use—fear as a mechanism for geopolitical social change, although it does not recognize that terrorism can be considered an overextension of a fear-based culture. Americans have a fear of casualties, military or civilian. The average American fear of casualties even during wartime is to some extent a mechanism which prevents the U.S. from actively exercising a formal expansionist agenda. The American economy has all the characteristics of a modern empire. Perhaps the lack of a formal agenda of expansion, combined with a reluctance to incur casualties, keeps the U.S. locked in its position as an empire in denial. It is interesting that the same fear of casualties served as Arafat's credo, which became a guiding principle in the PLO's thinking.[14]

Moral High Ground

Using a moral high ground as a foundation for foreign policy places the U.S. in a precarious position, as noted by Neil Livingstone: "The United States may yet perish as a nation of the delusion that it is necessary to be more moral than anyone else."[15] The danger in the Bush administration's morality-based rhetoric is that it confirms the American stereotypical doctrine of terrorism, and fuels the fears of Islamic fundamentalists who see globalization (Americanization) as a direct cause of the erosion of local values, traditions, cultures, and ideals. The erosion of the American image, portrayed as a religious and militaristic force set on molding the world in an image of itself, is not confined to emerging nations but is also becoming apparent with long-standing allies in Europe, where policy makers are putting a greater faith in the support and formation of international institutions to resolve global conflicts and stabilize economic regions.[16]

Consider, for a moment, terrorism as an emergent mentality which uses fear as a primary mechanism for geopolitical change. Next, consider the Bush administration's response: to seek out and smite the perpetrators of evil, regardless of location and in direct disregard for the sovereignty of any nation-state in which they may reside. Armed with a single-minded set of objectives, the United States is displaying a foreign policy behavior similar to that of business organizations looking for technological solutions as the primary means of exerting control, by injecting fear of job loss in the form of redundancies to motivate employees. Shoshana Zuboff points out the shortsightedness of this approach for corporations, which provides a striking parallel to that of national policy:

> *To concentrate only on intrinsic change and the texture of an emergent mentality is to ignore the real weight of history and the diversity of interest that pervade collective behaviour.*[17]

Where does it all end?

America is endeavoring to erect both physical and virtual walls to protect its borders from terrorist penetration. History indicates that isolationism leads only to the reinforcement of fear. The increase of walled communities in the U.S. to thwart crime creates the illusion of safe places. In reality, professional criminals can always penetrate those defenses. Isolated communities create fear and hatred of others, and over time, these places degenerate into havens of inequality and injustice; this happens in every city that responds to increased rates of violence by building more walled communities.[18] Is America moving swiftly toward becoming an island nation?

TWO

A New McCarthyism

History teaches that grave threats to liberty
often come in times of urgency, when constitutional
rights seem too extravagant to endure.
—*Justice Thurgood Marshall (1989)*

IS THE SEARCH FOR GLOBAL TERRORISM OR INDIVIDUALS WITH
potential terrorist tendencies a new version of McCarthyism? More
important, is the behavior of the U.S. administration post-9/11
a symptom of a long-standing but somewhat subdued culture of
paranoia? In 1966, Richard Hofstadter observed a pattern of paranoid overreaction that could be traced back to America's infancy,
when in 1798 a fear of subversion was linked to French Jacobeans
and pro-British monarchists.[19] During the administration of John
Adams, Congress passed the Alien and Sedition Acts, which tar-
geted aliens who had political ties with France because of a belief
that there were French spies in the United States. The acts granted
sweeping powers to arrest and deport any alien who was considered
dangerous and to prohibit publication of any materials that were
against the government. Thomas Jefferson and James Madison opposed the Sedition Act, writing laws in Kentucky and Virginia declaring that when the federal government oversteps the bounds of
the Constitution, the legislation is null and void. Resurgences of a

fear of foreigners and radicalism are also reflected in the actions toward freemasons in the early nineteenth century. Similarly, in the 1840s, fear led to actions against the Roman Catholic Church, and sparked anti-urbanization and anti-immigration movements.

There are many contemporary examples of America's fear that are based on irrationality under pressure rather than solid arguments; for example, Samuel Huntington's article, "José, Can You See," where the possibility of a massive Mexican immigration to the U.S. is portrayed as something extremely frightening to white Anglo Americans. This recurring rhetoric—where the "Other" is to be feared—has permeated U.S. society since the days of McCarthyism, manifesting today as racism, anti-Semitism, and anti-immigration.

It remains to be seen if the current line of neoconservative thinking—in which many seemingly disjointed activities are becoming linked to an antiterrorist agenda—evolves into another social phenomena like McCarthyism. What is more important is to understand the environment in which McCarthyism and fear are nourished. In 1950, senator Margaret Chase Smith wrote in her "Declaration of Conscience" speech:

> *Those of us who shout the loudest about Americanism in making character assassinations are all too frequently those who, by our own words and acts, ignore some of the basics principles of Americanism: the right to criticize; the right to hold unpopular beliefs; the right to protest; the right of independent thought.* [20]

Fifty years later, anyone who holds an opposite view from that of the administration, or who expresses an opinion contrary to that of the media, faces character assassination. They are summarily labeled as a conspiracy theorist, unpatriotic, or simply dismissed from the conversation. Vigilance must be applied when actions taken by government and nongovernment actors create the conditions in which public attitude leads to an erosion of civil rights.

The U.S. administration has a history of using a dialogue of fear as a tool to shape public opinion in the same way business uses fear in commercials to promote the purchase of a product or service. Indirect evidence of the public's fears, real or imagined, is captured in Franklin D. Roosevelt's famous address: "We have nothing to fear but fear itself." If one views the gross revenues of corporations directly and indirectly linked to the supply of security devices and services after 9/11, one can immediately note a sharp increase in sales to average citizens and new business customers. The market for home and business security worldwide is estimated at USD $231 billion, and it is projected to rise to USD $518 billion by 2015.[21] The protection market is booming during one of the sharpest economic downturns in recent memory. Fear, like sex, sells.

National security + public security.

The Enemy Within

Here we must examine how an external enemy becomes the enemy within by reviewing the fundamentals of how fear is used as an instrument of foreign and domestic policy, reelection campaigns, international trade, and transnational commerce. One example is how antiglobalizationists use fears such as job loss to offshore businesses in faraway countries as a rallying cry, while U.S. trade policies are designed specifically to retard equitable trade in favor of supporting long- and short-term American business interests. Another example is how immigrants are portrayed by the media as refugees looking for handouts, while in reality, many immigrants come with sufficient funds to start small businesses and other job-generating enterprises.

William Blum observes that American foreign policy, though often cloaked under a veil of morality, is designed to serve other imperatives. Blum defines these as

> . . . *making the world safe for American corporations by enhancing the financial statements of defense contractors at home who have contributed generously to members of Congress; preventing the rise of any society that might serve as a successful example of an alternative to the capitalist model; extending political and economic hegemony over as wide an area as possible, as befits a "great power." This in the name of fighting a supposed moral crusade against what Cold Warriors convinced themselves, and the American people, was the existence of an evil International Communist Conspiracy, which in fact never existed, evil or not.* [22]

The Bush administration's use of fear rhetoric as a basis for justifying its actions is strikingly similar to the justification and motivation used by the terrorists themselves, of a morality of just vengeance. [23] The Bush administration's preemptive foreign-policy communications send an all-too-familiar message to global citizens that still remember defining moments of the twentieth century in words uttered by one of Europe's former leaders, as noted by Linda Heard:

> *We have no interest in oppressing other people. We are not moved by hatred against another nation. We bear no*

grudge. I know how grave a thing war is. I wanted to spare our people such an evil. It is not so much the country, it is rather its leader. He has led a reign of terror. He has hurled countless people into the profoundest misery. We have displayed a truly exemplary patience, but I am no longer willing to remain inactive while this madman ill-treats millions of human beings.[24]

Of course, Heard was quoting Adolf Hitler, speaking on April 14, 1939, about Edward Benes, former president of Czechoslovakia. What should worry Americans is not how similar prewar Nazi rhetoric sounds when compared to the Bush administration's dialogue just before the invasion of Iraq, but how the rhetoric follows a pattern that can be viewed in the context of other historical events. This understanding of how a fear-based dialogue leads to national self-destruction and the erosion of liberty can best be described by examining two historical parallels in the 1790s and 1950s. One could argue that continued exploitation of the fear principle will ultimately lead to a resurgence of McCarthyistic activities by members of all parties within the political structure. McCarthyism, as we now call it, was a product of many years of cultivating a fear of subversion by communism—the "Red scare"—which reached a crescendo late in the process by the actions of Senator Joseph McCarthy. One must remember that the House of Representatives Special Committee on Un-American Activities (HUAC) existed long before McCarthy's action in 1950.

The pattern in which civil rights are slowly eroded is evident when examined under a lens of cause-and-effect in the context of the American society and its relationship with its elected leaders. Simply, an event occurs that increases the awareness of a certain condition by a select group or special interest. This awareness is synthesized into a threat to one of America's fundamental beliefs or principles, which in turn is used to promote the goals of the special interest group (including the military industrial complex and other government-linked activities). Once this awareness is acknowledged by increasing numbers of Americans, elected officials react quickly to pass legislation to thwart the perceived threat. In many cases, the reaction is an overreaction, which creates legislation that overcompensates for the real threat by catering to the perceived threat, and in the process tramples on the very rights of the citizens it purportedly acts to protect. Historically, many of these overreactive measures are themselves overturned or significantly reduced during subsequent decades; for example, the Alien and Sedition Act of 1790 and the Alien Registration Act (or Smith Act) of 1940. These acts granted federal government agencies sweeping and undefined authority with the express intent of identifying and seeking out subversives.

This raises yet another important question: Does the Patriot Act of 2001 go too far? On the surface, the almost zealous search for terrorists in all forms led by Congress and executed by a host of traditional and newly formed government agencies appears to follow the same pattern that eroded civil liberties in the 1790s and 1950s. How else is the U.S. using fear and threat as legitimization for defense?

THREE

The Romance of the Cold War

An intelligence service is, in fact, a stupidity service.
—E. B. White

THE FEAR OF AN ENEMY CAN BEST BE UNDERSTOOD UNDER THE rubrics of fear of a known threat, and fear of an unknown threat. The military provides a direct response to the fear of the known, while the U.S. intelligence service works to discover the unknown intentions of potential enemies. The fear associated with the Cold War was comfortable for Americans because it provided defined boundaries and a clear target. Global terrorism, on the other hand, is ubiquitous and without connection to any single nation-state, because it is based on religious and ideological principles. This type of threat is more difficult to thwart. The reassuring part of Cold War rhetoric was that it was designed to curtail enemy action by mutually assured destruction.

The intelligence service plays an interesting part in the continued promulgation of fear, as it supplies information, misinformation, intelligence, and analytical services to foreign policy makers. However, one must consider the motivations of these services, which failed to forecast Pearl Harbor, were unsuccessful at predicting the fall of the Berlin Wall, overestimated the USSR's capabilities, were surprised by 9/11, and provided faulty intelligence on

Saddam's weapons of mass destruction and other threats, both real and imagined. From a business perspective, an operating department with such a dismal record would find itself in a precarious position, having to prove to the organization its relative contribution to the value proposition of the firm.

This raises an important question: Is the network of intelligence services credible, effective, and useful as a source of information on which to base foreign policy? Or, should safeguards be developed to cross-reference and validate information before a reaction or preemptive action is taken? Not only are questions being raised on the information-gathering capabilities of the intelligence community, but flaws also exist in the dissemination of information by federal agencies. For example, the State Department's 2003 annual report on terrorism, *Patterns of Global Terrorism*, had to be reissued because it inadvertently reported that terrorism had fallen to a thirty-four-year low when in fact, it had risen sharply to a twenty-year high.[25]

During the Cold War, the consequences of actions often restricted the swiftness of reaction. Now the counterbalance of the Soviet threat has been removed. The actions of the Bush administration toward the UN as a regulator of relations between sovereign powers have blurred the defined boundaries of action and consequence, leaving us with a looming question: Who is the next enemy?

Admiral Eugene Carroll Jr., U.S. Navy (Ret.) vice president emeritus at the Center for Defense Information, makes an important observation: "For forty-five years of the Cold War we were in an arms race with the Soviet Union. Now it appears we're in an arms race with ourselves."[26] Now, according to Bush administration rhetoric—developed through many discourses by U.S. presidents, Democrats and Republicans alike—the evil empire lurks at every corner. Enemies are easily recognized by their failure to comply with U.S. intentions. This doctrine is compounded by the present-day process of gathering intelligence in association with other sovereign agencies, and is promising to be equally unreliable as made evident in the search for weapons of mass destruction in Iraq.

One could argue that according to this new pattern of identifying enemies by simply polling the intelligence community—and the subsequent justification of military action—nations such as Libya are at imminent risk of becoming the next enemy on the radar screen. Libyan leader Moammar Gadhafi may have sensed this, and moved cunningly to circumvent the new American posture by agreeing to allow international inspectors to check for all major weapons in the country, a step he said would be "of great importance" in stopping weapons of mass destruction in a global fight against terrorism.[27]

Using fear as a building block for foreign policy is not new. In 1933, Major General Smedley Butler clearly stated how the profits from war were attributed to maintaining a perceived threat encased in a rhetoric of nationalism, noting that the motivation for men to join the armed services was that "war [was] to make the world safe for democracy." In simple terms, General Smedley illustrated a key interrelationship between prewar industrial profits and the profits acquired as a direct result of World War I production. Corporate profit margins increased exponentially as patriotism fueled government spending, as reflected in the following figure.[28]

Government economists and military policy makers often point out a general decline in direct defense spending as a percentage of the Gross Domestic Product (GDP) over the last quarter-century.

	Profits 1910-1914	Profits 1914-1918
DuPont	6,000,000	58,000,000
Bethlehem Steel	6,000,000	49,000,000
US Steel	105,000,000	240,000,000
Anaconda	10,000,000	34,000,000
Utah Copper	5,000,000	21,000,000
Central Leather Co	3,500,000	15,000,000
General Chemical Co	800,000	12,000,000
International Nickel	4,000,000	73,000,000
American Sugar Refining Co	2,000,000	6,000,000
Source: Major General Smedley Butler, USMC, 1933		

Figure 2. American Corporate War Profits, 1910–1918.

However, this does not accurately reflect the shift in industrial output which has been refocused on the private sector. The same is true in the post-9/11 world, as the security industry has experienced a boom in revenues worldwide, growing from $55.6 billion in 1990 to an estimated $202 billion in 2010.[29] With fears of terrorism, criminals, and other social problems, revenues in the surveillance market have exploded. For example, shipments of Internet Protocol (IP) video surveillance cameras nearly doubled in 2005, and will continue to grow at a Compound Annual Growth Rate (CAGR) of 87.9 percent from 2004 to 2010, to reach an estimated U.S. $3.9 billion. To best understand the impact this one small example has on the U.S. economy, we can see that the exploding market for IP video surveillance cameras will generate an estimated U.S. $1 billion in semiconductors in 2010.[30] Surprisingly, one of the biggest potential markets for this technological surveillance is schools—where it will be used to prevent school violence, not terrorist acts.[31]

Without venturing into a detailed discussion on economics and military spending, we must consider that government purchases (military and nonmilitary alike) do not play the same role that they did in previous generations. The engine of government spending was previously the largest stimulus for economic growth. However, in the present time, it is merely a catalyst, one to be used in conjunction with other mechanisms to foster the momentum of economic activities.

Profiting from consumer fear is not new, as Dan Gillmor pointed out before 9/11:

> *Using fear to sell products is a time-honored, if somewhat unsavory, practice in our culture. Scare stories in the popular media—occasionally correct, often exaggerated—create the climate, and marketers take advantage. Entrepreneurs are leaping on public fears about online security, particularly when it comes to personal information.*[32]

Another example of the fear motive within industry, as we have mentioned, can be found in the years prior to 2000, where the computer industry publicized its concern over the Year 2000 "Millennium Bug" software problem, broadcasting fear of massive computer failures as consulting revenues soared.[33] Another more specific example can be found on the Internet site, "Sales Words Plus," which puts fear-based selling into an important context: "You may make a great truck brake, but it's *fear* that makes us actually get off the couch and purchase new brakes for the SUV that hauls the kids to school."[34]

All Types of Hazards

Today, corporations are profiting from the new fears generated by terrorism in the wake of 9/11. These businesses fall into three distinct categories: direct military suppliers; outsourced/indirect government contractors, such as civilian security services; and a host of security-based service companies generally labeled as emerging security industry organizations, which are simply fear opportunists.

To begin, we will briefly examine the fear opportunist merely in the context of how the behavior transfers in varying degrees into other categories. Two months after 9/11, in November 2001, the Federal Trade Commission, the Food and Drug Administration, and the California Department of Health Services investigated over two hundred Internet sites that were marketing bioterrorism-related products, including gas masks, protective suits, mail sterilizers, biohazard test kits, and homeopathic remedies and dietary supplements (with claims that the latter, including colloidal silver, zinc mineral water, thyme, and oregano oil are effective treatments for illnesses such as anthrax).[35] What is interesting about this third category (fear opportunists) is that it presents Americans with a paradox wherein it selectively prosecutes product-selling fear opportunists, as reported by the BBC: "Washington Attorney-General Christine Gregoire said state attorneys-general 'will not stand by while website operators capitalise on public fears by selling products that offer no protection.' "[36] Meanwhile, the government paved the way to support financial services firms selling terrorist insurance, which one could argue is simply a variation on the same theme.

However, within the first three categories, corporations that provide security services or cater to terrorist anxiety are typically engaged in products and services that can be seen as geared toward increasing personal safety. Within financial services companies and insurance firms, the offers focus squarely on terrorist insurance and other types of coverage, which has risen steadily since the tragic events of 9/11. Other types of postwar exploitation occur via legitimized government channels; for example, the U.S. military's biggest contractor in Iraq is Halliburton's Kellogg, Brown and Root, with estimated potential contracts of up to $18 billion in business. Halliburton was run by (now vice president) Dick Cheney, until he joined the race for the White House in 2000. A KBR analysis showed its subcontractors submitted bills based on estimates for the number of meals needed that were 19.4 percent higher than the actual number of meals that were served to troops at its twenty-seven dining centers.[37] In July 2002, Halliburton's stock was $10 per share; in February 2004, $34 per share, October 2007, $41 per share, with revenues rising from $16.2 billion in 2003 to $22.6 billion in 2006.

Make no mistake: Fear is a result of big business spawning economic activity across many industries. Panic over identity theft and threats to personal information security is fueling explosive growth of the biometrics market in the United States, estimated at U.S. $1.6 billion in 2007, and expected to grow to U.S. $5.3 billion by 2010.[38] The threat of terrorism and the ensuing fear it produces has since the 1980s been silently fueling the development of an ever-expanding personal security industry, which, one can argue, threatens to erode personal privacy and individual liberty.[39]

FOUR

Jihad Against Jews and Crusaders

"You can discover what your enemy fears most
by observing the means he uses to frighten you."
– Eric Hoffer (1902 – 1983)

On February 23, 1998, a group calling itself the "World Islamic Front" issued an edict against "Jews and Crusaders." This group included the now infamous Osama bin Laden, but also his subsequent number-two, Ayman al-Zawahiri, then of the Jihad organization in Egypt. Also signing up were the Jamiatul Ulema-e-Pakistan, and a similar jihadist movement in Bangladesh.

Published in an Arabic newspaper in London, it failed to get the attention it deserved, until after September 11, 2001. However, readers of *Foreign Affairs*[40] magazine were able to read what turned out to be a highly prescient article by Bernard Lewis, one that, if taken more seriously, could have possibly alerted the wider world to the magnitude of the danger it now faced.

Lewis did not transliterate the article in full, so here it is following the translation in Walter Laqueur's *Voices of Terror*.[41] While no two versions of the statement, or *fatwa*, are obviously identical, the meaning conveyed is very much the same. Here we are giving the fuller version, since its use of religious backing is highly germane to our concerns, especially the selective nature of the quotations from the Koran.

Praise be to Allah, who revealed the Book, controls the clouds, defeats factionalism, and says in his Book, "But when the forbidden months are past, then fight and slay the pagans wherever ye find them, seize them, beleaguer them and lie in wait for them in every stratagem of war." Peace be upon our Prophet, Muhammad bin Abdullah, who said, "I have sent the sword between my hands to ensure that no one but Allah is worshipped, Allah who put my livelihood under the shadow of my spear and who inflicts humiliation and scorn on those who disobey my orders."

The Arabian peninsula has never—since Allah made it flat, created its desert, and encircled it with seas—been stormed by any forces like the crusader armies spreading in it like locusts, eating its riches, and wiping out its plantations. All this is happening at a time in which nations are attacking Muslims like people fighting over a plate of food. In the light of [this] grave situation and the lack of support, we are obliged to discuss current events, and we should all agree on how to settle the matter.

No one argues today about three facts that are known to everyone. We will list them in order to remind everyone.

First, for over seven years the United States has been occupying the lands of Islam in the holiest of places, the Arabian peninsula, plundering its riches, dictating to its rulers, humiliating its people, terrorizing its neighbors and turning its bases in the peninsula into a spearhead through which to fight the neighboring Muslim peoples.

If some people in the past argued about the fact of the occupation, all the people of the peninsula have now acknowledged it. The best proof of this is the Americans' continued aggression against the Iraqi people, using the peninsula as a staging post, even though all its rulers are against their territories being used to that end, but they are helpless.

Second, despite the great devastation inflicted on the Iraqi people by the crusader-Zionist alliance, and despite the huge numbers of those killed, which has exceeded one million, despite all this, the Americans are once again trying to repeat the horrible massacres, as though they are not content with the protracted blockade imposed after the ferocious war or the fragmentation and devastation. So here they come to annihilate what is left of this people and to humiliate their Muslim neighbors.

Third, if the Americans' aims behind these wars are religious and economic, the aim is also to serve the Jews' petty state and to divert attention from its occupation of Jerusalem and the murder of Muslims there. The best proof of this is their eagerness to destroy Iraq, the strongest neighboring Arab state, and their endeavor to fragment all the states of the region such as Iraq, Saudi Arabia, Egypt and Sudan into paper statelets and through their disunion and weakness to guarantee Israel's survival and the continuation of the brutal crusade occupation of the peninsula.

All these crimes and sins committed by the Americans are a clear declaration of war upon Allah, his Messenger, and Muslims. And ulema [the official jurists able to interpret the Koran] have throughout Islamic history unanimously agreed that the jihad is an individual duty if the enemy destroys Muslim countries. This was revealed by Imam Bin-Qadamah in "Al-Mughni," Imam Al-Kisa'i in "Al-Bada'i," Al-Qurtubi in his interpretation, and the shaykh of Al-Islam in his books, where he said, "As for fighting to repulse [an enemy], it is aimed at defending sanctity and religion, and it is a duty as agreed [by the ulema]. Nothing is more sacred than belief except repulsing an enemy who is attacking religion and life."

On that basis, and in compliance with Allah's order, we issue the following fatwa to all Muslims:

The ruling to kill all Americans and their allies—civilians and military—is an individual duty for every Muslim who can do it in any country where it is possible to do it, in order to liberate the al-Aqsa Mosque and the holy mosque [Mecca] from their grip, and in order for their armies to move out of all the lands of Islam, defeated and unable to threaten any Muslims. This is in accordance with the words of Almighty Allah, "and fight the pagans all together as they fight you all together," and "fight them until there is no more tumult or oppression, and there prevail justice and faith in Allah."

This is in addition to the words of Almighty Allah: "And why should ye not fight in the cause of Allah and of those who, being weak, are ill-treated (and oppressed)?—women and children—whose cry is: "Our Lord, rescue us from this town, whose people are oppressors; and raise for us from thee one who will help!"

We—with Allah's help—call upon every Muslim who believes in Allah and wishes to be rewarded to comply with

Allah's order to kill the Americans and plunder their money wherever and whenever they find it. We also call upon Muslim ulema, leaders, youths and soldiers to launch the raid on Satan's U.S. troops and the devil's supporters allying with them, and to displace those who are behind them so that they may learn a lesson.

Almighty Allah said: "O, ye who believe, give your response to Allah and His Apostle, when He calleth you to that which will give you life. And know that Allah cometh between a man and his heart, and that it is He to whom ye shall all be gathered."

Almighty Allah also says: "O, ye who believe, what is the matter with you, that when you are asked to go forth in the cause of Allah, ye cling so heavily to the earth! Do ye prefer the life of this world to the hereafter? But little is the comfort of this life, as compared with the hereafter. Unless ye go forth, he will punish you with a grievous penalty, and put others in your place; but him ye will not harm in the least. For Allah hath power over all things."

Almighty Allah also says: "So lose no heart, nor fall into despair. For you must gain mastery if ye are true in faith."

Arguably, one can interpret *palingenetics*,[42] or *myth-based ultranationalism*, as a religious as well as purely secular phenomenon, and few better examples than this fatwa can be found. Bernard Lewis shows in his article "License to Kill: Osama Bin Laden's Declaration of Jihad"[13] that bin Laden and the others are referring principally to the three most sacred places in Islam. The first is the Arabian peninsula itself, where Islam originated. Next is present-day

Iraq, which was the core region of the great Abbasid caliphate; and, finally, he refers to Jerusalem, where Muhammad had one of his main visions, which is today commemorated in the Dome of the Rock. These are all geographical locations, whose physical defense is a duty to all true Muslims. In other words, we are not just talking about the global spiritual defense of a religion, but the physical and literal defense of its geographic sacred heartland territories.

All this is done on the basis of religion and the literal translation of sacred texts, not just from the Koran itself, but also from sayings of the Prophet and from the interpretations of leading members of the ulema. Bin Laden sees the world of Islam as a single national entity. While not all will agree with the interpretation we are following, one can see this as a religious use of Benedict Anderson's famous term, "imagined communities."[44]

Anderson, in his book of the same name, chiefly uses this construct to describe modern nations. In *Why the Nations Rage: Killing in the Name of God*,[45] Catherwood differs with him in ascribing the existence of the nation-state as a discrete entity to the modern period, agreeing instead with Anthony Smith's more persuasive *ethnie* theory,[46] that ethnic nationalism needs a more ancient origin than Anderson allows. Smith would concede to the modern nature of many of today's national boundaries, but nevertheless sees the core of numerous states going back far further into the past than the modern period, as argued elsewhere in this book. (The case is also argued convincingly from what Smith calls a *perennialist* viewpoint in Adrian Hastings's book, *The Construction of Nationhood: Ethnicity, Religion and Nationalism*).[47]

One of the great strengths of Anderson's theory is that he acknowledges the essentially Eurocentric approach of much of the current discussion on nationalism. Large swathes of today's "Two-

Thirds World" (formerly known as the Third World) suffers from entirely artificial boundaries, relics of the colonial period in which European administrators constructed multiethnic societies with little (if any) thought about the peoples living within the borders of the newly conquered regions. Much of the globe therefore lives in Anderson's *imagined communities*, with all the conflict that has, alas, taken place ever since.[48]

But one could also argue, using Anderson's model, that religious-based imagined communities exist as well, even if this is to take the original construct further than its creator did. Christendom as formerly understood, especially before the Reformation, is surely such a community. The boundaries of Western Christendom extended far beyond those of its core state, the Holy Roman Empire. The Papacy regarded its spiritual jurisdiction as covering the whole of Catholic Europe, and popes frequently intervened in the internal affairs of all European countries, such as when England, under King John in the early thirteenth century, found itself briefly under papal interdict. All those living in Christendom were regarded as Catholic Christians by dint of geography and birth. While Catholic Europe consisted of many different states, from Ireland in the West to Poland in the East, there was one recognized Christendom, and one Catholic faith.[49]

Islam, as understood by bin Laden and those Muslims of his persuasion, is the same. There is one *umma*, or community of the faithful, and one land of Islam, with Saudi Arabia as its sacred core. The world is divided into two—the *Dar al-Islam* and the *Dar al-Harb*. This twofold division of the world is religious; while many national boundaries exist within these two realms, the *real* split is based upon religion—those who are Muslims, and those who are not.[50]

As bin Laden put it on November 1, 2001: "The world has been divided into two camps: one under the banner of the cross, as Bush, the head of infidelity, said, and another under the banner of Islam."[51]

Take, for example, bin Laden's commentary on October 7, 2001, upon the results of the events of 9/11 that year:

> *I bear witness that there is no God but God [Allah in both instances in the original Arabic] and that Muhammad is his messenger. There is America, hit by God in one of its softest spots. Its greatest buildings were destroyed . . . thank God for that. What America is tasting now is something insignificant compared to what we have tasted for scores of years. Our nation has been tasting this humiliation and this degradation for more than eighty years.*[52]

In the *Guardian* translation of this declaration, the words "[Islamic World]" were added by way of explaining the term "our nation" to Western readers.[53] This is correct, since radical Islam sees the whole world of the Muslim umma as the equivalent of a single, Islamic, nation.

As bin Laden continues:

> *These events have divided the whole world into two sides. The side of believers and the side of infidels, may God keep you away from them. Every Muslim has to rush to make his religion victorious. The winds of faith have come. The winds of change have come to eradicate oppression from the island of Muhammad, peace be upon him.*[54]

On October 10, 2001, Al-Qaeda issued a similar fatwa, in relation to the American decision to root out the Taliban and bomb Afghanistan.[55]

The "more than eighty years" is also significant. What bin Laden refers to here is the fall of the Ottoman Empire, whose rulers, the sultans, had granted themselves the old Islamic title of "caliph," in abeyance since the time of the Abbasid caliphs. The Ottoman Empire itself was abolished in 1922, and the separate, religious, title of "caliph" two years later, in 1924, ironically at the behest of a Muslim ruler, President Kemal Ataturk, of Turkey.[56]

Until that time, while most Muslims had actually lived outside Ottoman territory, notably in British-ruled India and Dutch East Indies (now Indonesia), Sunni Muslims all around the world had, in some way, acknowledged the religious suzerainty of the caliph. It was fear of how Muslims under British rule in India and Egypt would react to Britain being at war that helped to lead the United Kingdom in World War I to support the so-called "Arab Revolt" against Ottoman rule a rebellion (notionally, at least) led by a descendant of Muhammad himself, Emir Feisal of the Hashemite clan.[57]

In the end it was the Turks themselves who abolished the caliphate, and despite the attempts of various Muslim rulers since then to claim the title, it has never been successfully resurrected. Restoration of a fully Islamic caliphate has, instead, become one of the great rallying cries of radical Islamist groups, from Al-Qaeda to various similar groups as far afield as Uzbekistan.

For them, such a restored caliphate is an integral part of their desire to bring Islam back to the purity of the seventh century, the era of the Four Rightly Guided Caliphs, all of whom were also Companions of the Prophet.

However, all but one of these original caliphs died violently. Furthermore, since the caliphate of Ali, Muhammad's son-in-law, led to the eventual and permanent split of Islam into its current Sunni and Shiite divisions, the early decades of Islamic history cannot really be said to have been as golden in reality as they seem now to many in retrospect. These foundational decades have, to some, been bathed in a mythic glow, as an ideal era of how Islamic polity should—and did—work. They are also mythical in the heroic sense, since they represent military success for Islam that not even the Ottoman Empire was able to repeat, even at its height. By the time of the Umayyad caliphs, based in present-day Syria, the world of the Islamic umma stretched without interruption from today's Spain in the West to the furthest eastern boundaries of twenty-first-century Iran in the East. No power seemed as great as that of the Islamic caliphate. All the criteria for a myth of a Golden Age are fulfilled,[58] especially in terms of the early Muslim triumphs.

As a result, the employment of the term *palingenetics*—or myth-based ultranationalism—would be more than appropriate to the *salafiyya*, or ancestor-admiring school of Islamic thought of which Al-Qaeda is the modern embodiment, *salaf* being the Arabic for "ancestor." (Here it is important to note, as Akbar Ahmed and others remind us, that the original, late-nineteenth-century version of *salafiyya* was very different—thoughtful, moderate Muslims trying to work out how to remain Muslim and at the same time bring genuine Islam into compatibility with modernity.)[59]

Imagined Communities and Beyond

Understood as a nation, radical Islam can thus be said to have created an imagined community, a single entity with a sacred geographic core, with its own palingenetic vision to be defended by force, and at all costs.

This definition brings this version of Islam alongside the equally palingenetic *Hinduvta* version of nationalistic Hinduism, the similar *Eretz Israel* beliefs of hard-line Jews, and the Christian identity notions of survivalist groups who perceive America as being a special, white, Christian nation. For all these movements, territoriality remains at the heart of their religious beliefs, a powerful concept of sacred space, along with foundational myths regarded as a Golden Age that needs to be recovered if both power and purity are to be restored.

Muslims of all stripes, moderates included, have expressed nostalgia for the Golden Age of the Umayyad caliphate of al-Andalus.[60] But the fact remains that such a place was one in which the great Jewish philosopher Maimonides could thrive, away from the anti-Semitic lands to the north of Western Christendom. This must surely be proof that the reality of that more-tolerant Golden Age can legitimately be an inspiration for moderate twenty-first-century Muslims, happy to live in peace alongside those of the other two Abrahamic faiths. But it is hard to see how it could motivate those of the *salafiyya* variety, for whom tolerance of any kind is anathema.

So, to Osama bin Laden and those of like mind, there are two kinds of people—those with us (the *Dar al-Islam*, or Realm of Islam), and those against us (the *Dar al-Harb*, or Realm of War). Does this sound familiar? Perhaps it should . . . .

Moderate Muslims, of whom there are many (especially in the U.S.), have other categories. Some believe in the Realm of Truce (*Dar al-Sulh*), and others, better still, the *Dar al-Salaam*, which is not just the name of the Tanzanian capital but also a concept—

the Realm of Peace. Either way, the moderate way forward is to increase the number of options open to faithful Muslims, away from the confrontational approach—Islamic Caliphate vs. Infidel Enemy—toward other possibilities, such as living happily in a state of truce (*sulh*), or, even better, actually at peace (*salaam*).

But this is more complex and not open to oversimplification. A fear-engendered approach is a much easier one for many to comprehend: There are bad guys and good guys, and if we don't get them first, they will get us. Anything else is hard work!

So how does all this relate to foreign policy, clashing civilizations, and the threat of terror?

FIVE

Religion and the Rationale for Violence

Fear can make a donkey attack a lion.
—*Arab Proverb*

On February 2, 2003, *The New York Times* ran a story entitled "The Other Face of Fanaticism: While the West Worries over Islamic Fundamentalism, India's Hindu Nationalists Thrive by Stirring Up a Murderous Anti-Muslim Frenzy."[61] The importance of this cannot be overestimated. After 9/11, the tendency has been to blame religious terror on Muslim fanatics, as the article implies, and forget that other religions are also responsible for much of the terrorism in our twenty-first-century world. Muslims are not just perpetrators, but victims too. With the tsunami disaster of December 2004, we were all reminded that one of the affected areas, Sri Lanka, has seen a long and bloody struggle between Buddhists and Hindus, an ethnic and religious war in which Muslims have played no part. We hope here to redress the balance, by looking at killers of many religions, and possible causes for their actions. At the heart of much of the murder is the issue of self-identity.

In other words, Westerners are not the only target of hatred; enemies also exist within the attackers' own societies. A major source of Western fear after 9/11 was that there were millions of people "out there" who hated "us here" for reasons we could not begin to understand. Who can possibly hate people as nice as Americans, after all?

Now, of course, there are also plenty of self-critical folk in the U.S. who realize that their country is not perfect, can be seen as tactless or even imperialistic, and therefore sometimes deserving of the criticism directed at it by people overseas. But even here, too, such self-critics put far too much emphasis on the U.S., or on the West. It never occurs to them that the motivation for those attacking the West could be as much to do with internal conflicts within their own societies as it is some kind of visceral hatred against the West, or the U.S. in particular. In addition, much of the hatred seems to be of a symbolic kind; it is not so much America per se that they hate, but what it stands for and what that means in relation to what is happening in their own countries.

So it is not so much *us* that they hate as things in their home countries, and within themselves as individuals living in rapidly changing societies. That is not to say that hatred of the USA plays no role, but that Americanophobia is amongst the causes and not always the main motivation. American multinational expansionism is an easy target because it is a clearly discernible enemy. In reality it is easier to place blame for changes in the fabric of society (modernity) on an external force such as American business interest rather than examining the root cause of internal societal strife. For example, McDonald's is a profit oriented business and is often criticized for imposing itself on traditional communities. Yet there has never been one reported incident of someone being dragged off the streets into McDonald's and forced to eat a hamburger at gunpoint. If a local commuity does not want McDonald's (Wal-Mart or any other multinational) simply stop eating there or stop buying their products. As a for profit enterprise they will simply leave if they can not generate profits. So the people to blame are one's neighbors for buying or eating, but that is a much more difficult reality to contemplate. The same tenet is true for America with its self-made fear of job loss from foreign entities as they continue to consume foreign goods. Clearly, as we will see, things like the war in Iraq don't help, but nor are such things the sole cause of conflict.

In examining the issue of self-identity and religious groups, we must consider the important theories of Vamik Volkan, in his work, *Bloodlines: From Ethnic Pride to Ethnic Terrorism*,[62] and those of Indian psychologist, Sudhir Kakar. What is extraordinary to many of us is that a key rationale for terrorism is that the values of the society from which the terrorists come are under attack from external malign forces, principally seen as Westerners and their values. Much of the world feels under siege, and it is precisely this mentality that leads people to react by committing terrorism against the West.

As we have noted, it is not always the West that is the enemy. While Hindus in Bangalore might destroy their local McDonald's—on the basis that, although McDonald's is carefully vegetarian in India, it nevertheless embodies Western capitalist values—the Muslim minority is increasingly the object of extremist Hindu hatred and violence as well. In examining religious violence worldwide, this is not something that we should omit.

The battle of Kosovo was a Serb defeat, and one could say that for the Serbs to celebrate it every year is not unlike the British holding an annual commemoration for Bunker Hill, or the French remembering Trafalgar and Waterloo. But it is in its psychic importance that the battle and the cult surrounding it becomes truly important—and revealing.

Vamik Volkan describes such negativity in terms of an "ethnic tent."[63] In such circumstances, groups can behave like individuals if they perceive their tent as being threatened. When our core character is formed, not all aspects of our personality get integrated properly. We either try to sweep these unintegrated parts of ourselves under the carpet—*repression*—or externalize them in things or people outside ourselves. This latter way of dealing with our unintegrated self is called *projection*, and we see this in all the different forms of terrorism mentioned in this book.

Religious or ethnic groups can choose an event as a central trauma that is common to all of them and use it as projection against a common enemy. Volkan uses the Serb obsession with the battle of Kosovo as such an example:

> *Adopting a chosen trauma can enhance ethnic pride, reinforce a sense of victimization, and even spur a group to avenge its ancestors' hurts . . . As the image of the Battle of Kosovo and its Serb heroes [was] kept alive throughout six centuries, the story became a frequent and significant subject for countless artistic impressions. It emerged and continues to emerge in icons, folk songs, poems, paintings . . . like a religious symbol that supports the Serbs sense of being a "chosen people." By holding on to the memory of the Battle of Kosovo, when manipulated by their leaders following the collapse of the former Yugoslavia, Serbs also fueled a shared feeling of entitlement to revenge, which sanctioned official propaganda and atrocities.[64]*

This feeling of victimhood was used to justify terrible atrocities. These did not begin with the massacres, mass rapes, and incarcerations in concentration camps familiar to us from our television screens in the 1990s, but go back much further. The Serb atrocities are examples of religious terror, as are Islamic attacks upon the West, or intrareligious murder, such as the assassination of Prime Minister Rabin; all of these are religiously motivated terrorist attacks. Apart from anything else, it is also important for people in the West to realize that Muslims are often, as in Bosnia, Kosovo, and India, victims as well as perpetrators.

A classic example of projection is the way in which Bosnian Muslims and Kosovar Albanian Muslims alike are seen as "Turks."[65] Ethnically speaking, as many writers on the subject have demonstrated, the actual ethnic differences between Serb, Croat, and Bosnian are minute. Similarly, Albanians are ancient inhabitants of the Balkan peninsula, fully European from time immemorial, and all this despite the conversion of many, centuries ago, to the Muslim faith of the medieval Ottoman Turkish invaders. Whatever religion these groups may have adopted, they are all Europeans, and in the case of the Bosnian Muslims, fellow Slavs of their Serb and Croat neighbors.

Yet to many of those committing atrocities against them, from the eighteenth century through the late twentieth, these, their fellow Slavs, were "Turks," part of the alien overlord race which ruled most of the Balkans from roughly the fourteenth century through the early twentieth (with much of the region gaining its independence during the nineteenth).

When Fear Goes Too Far

What shocked many observers during the mass killings of the 1990s was the fact that people of different religious groups had been raised together, frequently in the same, or in neighboring, towns and villages. But a quotation from 1992 from a young Serb militia man is revealing: "I have cut the throats of three Turks so far, and I don't even have nightmares." [66]

Many people were equally stunned, for example, that Radovan Karadzic, the leader of the Bosnian Serbs during the worst of the massacres there, from 1992 through 1995, was a trained psychologist. Advocates of Hindu violence in India have similarly often been university graduates. It should not surprise us, though, since outside of the increasingly secular West, brains and belief are by no means incompatible.

Sayyid Qutb, the Egyptian writer and thinker, has been called "the leading ideologue of the jihadist movement." [67] Qutb was put to death on the orders of Egyptian leader Gamal Abdel Nasser in 1966, after becoming famous for the Islamic work, *Signposts Along the Road*.[68] His views, so inspirational to Atta and the other 9/11 terrorists, are also a classic example of projection. Using the kind of analysis employed by Vamik Vulkan, one can argue that Qutb and those Islamists of his stripe see the Islamic world as being threatened by the West. This is important in terms of the violence that extremist Islamic terrorists employ, for, as we shall see, they state that *jihad* is lawful in defense in a way that is not allowed in aggression. If the *Dar al-Islam* is under attack, then violence may legitimately be used in its defense, as it was, for example, in New York, Bali, Madrid, and London.

Both Qutb and many of the 9/11 hijackers had lived in the West. They came from prosperous, middle-class backgrounds. Qutb lived in several places in the U.S. when there on a teaching scholarship. It was at an innocent church dance in Greeley, Colorado, where he noticed men and women dancing together, that he became appalled by what he perceived to be the decadence of the West. Atta, similarly, lived for many years in Hamburg, Germany, as did some of the other 9/11 leaders. What is surely significant is that these people, well-educated, intelligent, professional Egyptians, became jihadists perhaps precisely *because* they had lived in the West. (While *jahiliyya*—igorance—is an an important category for Qutb and similar writers, so too is the term *hakimiyyah*.[69] This is difficult to translate, since it can mean different things depending on the context. Normally it entails *sovereignty*, but in the case of writers such as Qutb, it perhaps means *divine sovereignty*, the absolute rule of Allah, as opposed to the man-made rule Qutb so disliked in Nasser's Egypt.)

While it is possible to exaggerate the role that fear of Western infiltration plays in forming worldviews, Middle East scholar Bernard Lewis is surely right to say that in Islam, it is significant that part of the lure of the "Great Satan" is that Satan is a seducer.[70] There is much that is attractive in the West that is at the same time firmly contrary to the values of Islam. What repels us is often something that simultaneously draws us, and this is true of the temptations of the West.

So perhaps the fact that Qutb, Atta, and others hated the West after having lived in it should not surprise us as much as it does. We want to destroy things that both attract and disgust us because their destruction brings resolution to our inner conflict, and, as we have seen from many recent atrocities, thousands across the world may have died because of the inner torment of intelligent, well-educated men and the way in which they projected that personal struggle onto the external enemy, the West.

Qutb's principle that *jihad* may be used because the Islamic world is under attack is the rationale for extremist attacks upon the

West. When it comes to definitions of *jihad*, there is no consensus in the world of experts, Muslim or Western.[71] One suspects that on this thorny topic, the individual writer's *a priori* view of Islam determines how *jihad* is interpreted, whether the violent or peaceful interpretation is the one that is used. Suffice it to say here that authors such as Daniel Pipes[72] are perhaps being unfair when they pronounce that the *real* Islamic doctrine of *jihad* is that of violent holy war, and that Muslims who think otherwise are dissembling. Well-meaning Western professors, of the kind that Pipes criticizes,[73] who claim that *all* Muslims have renounced violent holy war as an option, are, as Pipes claims, mistaken. From Qutb to bin Laden, plenty of Muslims have, alas, taken the path of war. But those countless Muslims who believe *jihad* in the twenty-first century to be a wholly pacific doctrine of personal spiritual growth and development, are equally sincere and equally Muslim!

In classic Muslim doctrine, *jihad* may not even be warfare at all.[74] The *greater jihad* is the inward struggle to be a better Muslim, a Sufi-inspired belief as near as Islam gets to the Christian doctrine of sanctification and *spiritual* (as opposed to literal) warfare. Many reform-minded and moderate Muslims today recognize the greater jihad as the only legitimate form now on offer, and that the days of holy war have long since departed. Physical, actual war, in terms of battles, the *lesser jihad*, is now over.[75]

However, the Koran *does* allow for fighting in defense of the lands of Islam, and it is this excuse that Qutb and those of his ilk use to justify attacks upon those who are themselves attacking Islam.[76]

What is significant about not just Qutb but also about the rise of religious Islamic extremism in general is that it has become popular since the perceived failure of Arab socialist nationalism, of the kind espoused in particular by Nasser in the 1950s and 1960s.

As we see elsewhere, both socialism and *ethnic* nationalism (as opposed to its religious variety) are imports from the West. The massive psychological shock of the defeat in the 1967 war against Israel was the chance that the radical Islamists needed to win converts to their cause.

As an Eyptian political prisoner wrote in 1967: "Israel and Nasser were both, for them, but two variants of tyranny, both totally inimical to Islam."[77]

To Qutb, under tyrants like Nasser, "man is under the domination of man rather than of Allah."[78] Furthermore, and this is also important in Qutb's thinking, "everything around is *jahiliyyah*, . . . including a good part of what we consider Islamic culture."[79] People could, as Nasser did, profess Islam, but not be proper Muslims at all. This is vital to grasp; it is the basis upon which Qutb and his disciples felt able to attack those who, for all their profession to Islam, were not deemed to be real Muslims according to a strict interpretation of the faith.

So to Qutb, the Pan-Arab doctrines of Nasser and his kind (in Syria, Iraq, and elsewhere) were rejected,[80] since that would allow non-Muslim Arabs, such as Palestinian Christians—not to mention the Syrian Christian founder of the Ba'ath Party, Michel Aflaq—as equals. As Qutb put it, the "sole collective identity Islam offers is that of the faith."[81] This, today, is the difference between the PLO, which is secular, albeit overwhelmingly Muslim, and Hamas and Hezbollah, that are specifically Islamic and closed to Christians.

Qutb rejected geographical nationalism in favor of the religious kind:

> *The homeland a Muslim should cherish and defend is not a mere piece of land; the collective identity he is known by is*

not that of a regime . . . His jihad is solely geared to protect the religion of Allah and his Sharia and to save the abode of Islam and no other territory.[82]

When questioned by Nasser's security police on why he was not an Arab patriot, Qutb retorted, "Patriotism should consist in bonds to the faith, not to a piece of land. The present, territorial, sense given to this term should be greatly stretched."[83] To Qutb, and similar writers in Pakistan, Muslims had forgotten their Islamic past.[84] The "modern *jahiliyya*,"[85] or living in the days of unbelief, was profoundly unhelpful to his fellow Muslims, and explained the defeatist attitude in which many of them lived.[86]

This is vitally important to our concerns, because what we are seeing in the Muslim world is not so much a Muslim war against the West, but *a war within Islam for the control of that religion.* In other words—"they" might hate us, but they hate fellow Muslims of the wrong sort a good deal more than they hate infidels like us in the West.

Sunni Muslims do not normally believe in revolt against legitimate rulers, for fear of strife, or to use the Arabic term, *fitna.* But as Emmanuel Sivan has pointed out, "The task Sayyid Qutb set for himself was to legitimise revolt in terms of mainstream Sunni thought. He had, in a word, to ban the specter of *fitna.*"[87]

Much of this thinking is based upon mythic ages past; in the case of the *salafiyya* school of Islam, on the existence of the golden age of the first four caliphs; and in the case of *hindutva*, of a pure India under Hindu rulers, before the Muslims invaded. One could call this *myth-based ultranationalism palingenetics.*

Of Religions and Nations

Radical Islam, political Hinduism, and extremist Judaism and Christianity, are all actual rather than mere substitute religions. If myth-based ultranationalism can legitimately apply to an ersatz belief such as Nazism, it should also be able to apply to the radical elements of genuine religions. Religion, as Anthony Smith so clearly demonstrates, is frequently at the heart of a nation's core myth. In particular, Smith shows, "salvation religions" prove to be the longest-lasting. While no one today worships Zeus, Christianity, Islam, Judaism, and Hinduism have all endured.

A link between religion and nationalism exists in all four of these salvation faiths. In Western Europe, the link between a geographical territory and religious zeal was broken in the years between the origins of the Protestant Reformation in 1517, and the Treaty of Westphalia that ended the Thirty Years War in 1648. Ever since the latter time, twentieth- and twenty-first-century historians and political scientists have referred to the "Westphalian System." Wars of religion, and in the case of France in the sixteenth century, civil religious wars, were now a thing of the past.

The Westphalian system, in *realist* political and international relations theory, refers to the primacy of the state and of state interests as the primary unit in dealings between countries. It presupposes that states are the prime international "actors," and that each state acts primarily in its own national/secular interests. That is not to say that ideology is irrelevant. Nazi Germany and Soviet Russia acted as much in the interests of fascism and communism respectively as in purely German or Russian national considerations. But it is also true to add, for example, that Hitler and Stalin regarded their respective ideologies as being in the interests of their respective countries. Further, although both men were dictators, they used nation-states as the prime means of projecting their respective beliefs. The concept of the primacy of the state was not affected.

But one can also argue that this is a very Eurocentric way of looking at the world. We now live in an age of *religious nationalism*—a subject upon which Mark Juergensmeyer of UC Santa Barbara has written several helpful books which it is possible to read without possessing a political science degree—and that is how we now have religious fanatics in Afghanistan, such as Al-Qaeda, launching attacks on a country as far away as America. In the new warfare, old national boundaries are no longer important.

So we can come full circle to the question: Who hates us, and why?

This is a complex issue, and not quite as simple as some people make out. To those who have followed President Bush, it is a war against America, or against the West. At this writing, Bush has been urging people to support him in Iraq in the name of the war against terror. But, if the war in Islam is not Islam vs. the West, but different Islamic groups against each other—as we see in Iraq, where thousands of Iraqis are killed *by other Iraqis* or by Arab Islamic militants using Iraq as their post-Afghanistan training ground—we simply cannot say this. In fact, one could argue that other Muslims are in far more danger than we are in the West, especially if we follow the advice that Ibn Taymiyya gave to the rulers of Egypt of his own time—that apostates are worse than infidels.

Much of this came up in Britain after the failed terrorist attacks in London, and in Glasgow in 2007. Serious television programs debated the battle *within* Islam, and thinking Muslims such as Akbar Ahmed and Benazir Bhutto (the two-time and first woman prime minister of Pakistan) took part in the discussions. As Ahmed made clear, much of the hatred ordinary Muslims feel is directed toward their *own* leaders, many of whom, he points out, are undemocratic and dictatorial. As Bhutto reminded us, there have been, in Pakistan, attacks by Sunni Muslims on Shiite mosques, and, inevitably, revenge Shia attacks on Sunnis.

One of the most thoughtful articles was by a former jihadist Muslim, now turned filmmaker, Shiraz Maher. As Maher reminds us, in a piece in the *New Statesman*, it is not a case of Islam versus the West, of the kind that some of the neoconservatives and others in the U.S. have been arguing. Rather, as he shows, ". . . contrary to conventional wisdom, terrorism is not about simple retaliation for perceived grievances. Islamist violence in the West is invariably linked with a desire to see the realization of a worldview."[88] The article points out that violent Muslims are not killing us because of our foreign policy or because they hate the West, but because they are trying to impose what Maher calls a "puritanical caliphate" upon the world in accordance with their religious interpretation of Islam. At the same time President Bush was appearing on television to say that keeping U.S. forces in Iraq was making the West safe from terrorism. This fearmongering has been an important part of his policy generally. But if what Maher and other refugees from extremist Islam are telling us—and they are convincing in what they say—then Bush and others have got it totally wrong, as have folk like "Anonymous," the famous former CIA operative later outed as Michael Gruer, who also, albeit far more intelligently and cogently, expresses the view that our actions make a difference to extremist Islam.

The issue is best summarized by an adaptation of a theme by *Washington Post* journalist Thomas Friedman, best known for his famous books on globalization and its consequences. He adopts the perspective of Middle Eastern journalist, Rami Khouri: the *Arab Street* vs. the *Arab Basement*. One could, along with the pundits of BBC programs such as *Newsnight*, take this one stage further and look at the *Islamic Street* and the *Islamic Basement*. In either analogy, the Basement houses the extremists—the people who really do want to kill us. But, as we have seen, these are people whose ideology, following Qutb, and before him, Wahhab and Ibn Taymiyya, is primarily *religious*. They are using violence for religious ends, for the restoration of the ideal Islamic rule of the early centuries of that faith, and of the Golden Age of the Islamic caliphate in particular, when Islam was the predominant world power.

However, the Basement needs recruits, and here is where Gruer (Anonymous) and others do have a point, although they may not have the full picture. Islamic extremists have long talked of the Near Enemy—the regime in Egypt being the prime example, from Qutb onward, and the Far Enemy being the U.S. and other Western countries, whose aid props up such regimes, like that of Mubarak, today. As we have just seen, the *prime* enemy, according to Qutb, is the *Near* Enemy, since they are regimes that ought to be truly Islamic and are not. It is their removal that is the ultimate aim.

But we in the West are, many now argue, playing into the hands of the extremists—the Basement—by our foolishness, and this is where Gruer and others are correct. For the Street does not believe in the necessity of a caliphate, or in the full dogmas of extremist Islam. They do, however, care about their fellow Muslims, and, in today's mass communication age, they can see Palestinians being oppressed (as they interpret it) or regimes that profess to be Islamic, such as that of Iraq, being invaded by the West, even though Saddam was more secular than Islamic. They note that military dictatorships, such as those of Mubarak in Egypt and

Musharraf in Pakistan, are supported strongly and to the tune of billions of dollars of aid by Western governments, who at the same time profess the desire to install democracy in the Middle East. The Street *is* angry at what they perceive to be Western hypocrisy, and what they interpret—however false the perception—as Western antipathy toward Islam.

As Maher and similar former extremists point out, this is not the rationale of the Basement—the people who actually want to and sometimes, tragically, succeed in killing us. But the Basement needs to recruit from somewhere, and their source is the angry and disillusioned members of the Street. So, unfortunately for us in the West, American policy has played straight into the hands of the Basement, by enraging the Street. The paradox of the Bush position, as countless books on Iraq have reminded us, is that in trying to make America safer, Bush has actually made the world a far more dangerous place. Implementing an invasion of Iraq, a country in which the extremists were ruthlessly suppressed—despite Cheney's strange tales to the contrary—in turn has created a wonderful recruitment ground for the Basement by angering the Street and by creating an insurgency that has replaced Afghanistan as the training ground for modern jihadist guerrilla groups. (And here we must remember again: *Most killing in Iraq is one group of Muslims killing another, not Westerners*—so much so, in fact, that at this writing, it appears that some anti-American Sunni tribal leaders are now helping Americans because they are so shocked at the sheer violence and extremism of the jihadi groups.)

Thus, ironically, a president who has used fear for his own political ends, as we will now see, has created a global climate in which we now need to fear where we did not before, because he has caused dangers to the West that were hitherto nonexistent. So

let us now go on to look at part of the disastrous legacy of fear created in recent years, not forgetting the important point we saw in
the other chapters—that George W. Bush is not the first president
to have done something like this, nor is he likely to be the last.

Part II:
The U.S. Fear/Threat Reaction and Global Defense

So first of all let me assert my firm belief that the
only thing we have to fear . . . is fear itself . . . nameless,
unreasoning, unjustified terror which paralyzes needed
efforts to convert retreat into advance.
—*Inaugural Speech of Franklin Delano Roosevelt*
(Washington, D.C., March 4, 1933)

IN TODAY'S CLIMATE, PERHAPS ROOSEVELT'S QUOTE HAS BEEN rewritten to "We have nothing but fear in fear itself" or as Norman Solomon, Executive Director of the Institute of Public Accuracy put it: "the only thing we have to fear is not having enough fear." Just as George W. Bush has declared war on global terrorism, Franklin D. Roosevelt declared war on despair, realizing that in the aftermath of the stock market meltdown of 1929, which left the country and the banking industry in a state of economic collapse, a massive increase in government spending would be the only solution to restart the U.S. economy. Franklin D. Roosevelt's intent was simply to make the government the employer of necessity long enough to get the economy growing. Public works programs from building dams, reforestation, public art (murals), road construction, and numerous other highly visible projects were engineered to restore the nation's self-esteem.

It would be naive to simply compare the 1930s economic condition and the use of government spending with the economic climate of the early 2000s. However, significant parallels can be found:

- World War I ends in 1918, approximately ten years of prosperity, market collapse 1929, followed by economic depression and isolationism

- Cold War ends in 1989, approximately ten years of prosperity, dot-com stock market crash in 2000, followed by economic recession and isolationism

The U.S. reaction to the events of 9/11 was foreseeable, as legislators moved into law new regulations that would thwart any repeat attempts by terrorists to use the same means to terrorize again. This, of course, underestimates the resourcefulness of terrorists, as it neglects to consider that they would be more likely to approach the problem using different means. Added airport security, a revamping of immigration controls, and more invasive financial regulations are reminiscent of the steps taken by the U.S. during the post–McCarthy era and throughout the Cold War, in which America labored under the misinformation supplied by the intelligence community. Now, the American technological superiority ushers in a new age of geography-free commerce, coupled with an instantaneous exchange of funds, capital, and payments, heralding a new era of free trade and easy-to-acquire foreign direct investment. However, this new economic vision comes complete with a new world order handcrafted by the U.S. administration, in which nation-states fall into two clear categories: nations that agree, and nations that are allied with the axis of evil, rhetoric strikingly similar to the anticommunist doctrine of the administration during the 1950s and '60s. As Chalmers Johnson notes that the American military-industrial complex began to seek out a new enemy because the administration could not conceive of dismantling an economy that depended on sustained military spending. To put U.S. military spending into context Johnson reminds us that: "according to the Defense Department's annual *Base Structure Report* for fiscal year 2003, which itemizes foreign and domestic U.S. military real estate, the Pentagon currently owns or rents 702 overseas bases in 130 countries and has another 6,000 bases in the United States and its territories."

In the post–Cold War era, the United States developed a unique sense of global self awareness, moving into areas of global instability while working within an international legal framework it helped to establish following World War II. However, the Bush administration's preventive strike doctrine raises an important question of whether international laws are still valid, as non-state actors (such as globally coordinated terrorists) begin to play a larger role in shaping world events.[89] It is easy to criticize the Bush administration's posture toward the United Nations' role in defensive peacekeeping. Tomas Valasek, for example, argues that the fundamental structure of the world has changed in three key ways: non-state actors are playing a larger role; failing or failed states with or without a central government, with a government that controls only a portion of the state's territory, or with several competing governments unable to control large parts of its own territory, unintentionally create havens for terrorist organizations;

and the technological nature of the threat is changing the definition of self-defense.[90] The United Nations' role as a negotiator and regulator of relations between sovereign powers is ineffective with failing nation-states or non-state actors, as seen in the Palestine/Israel tension.

SIX

Ethnic Tents and Nationalist Hatreds: The Need for Enemies

It is not death or pain that is to be dreaded,
but the fear of pain or death.
—*Epictetus*

WHERE WERE YOU ON SEPTEMBER 11, 2001?

For the generation born after the murder of John F. Kennedy in 1963 or the first moon landing in 1969, this has become *the* question to ask, since people around the world, let alone in the United States, all remember where they were and what they were doing when they saw the planes hit the Twin Towers on that infamous day.

As authors, we clearly remember that day. Joseph was in the Russian embassy in London, where he was quickly escorted out of the building by men in dark suits and sunglasses without being given a reason for the expulsion. Making his way to the London underground, a large crowd of people in front of the electronics shop, with faces unmoving, intently watching the television, drew his attention. Meanwhile, Christopher was in Charlottesville, Virginia, recuperating in his apartment from a serious injury that had occurred just a few days earlier. His wife phoned him from

England to say that she was watching the horrors on BBC news. Quickly he switched on the television and spent the next two days glued to the screen as the horrific scenes unfolded.

Everyone still refers to the days immediately after 9/11 as those when the world changed. Few dare to challenge that consensus. (One of the rare authorities who did was Sir Michael Howard, the preeminent British historian and cofounder of the International Institute of Strategic Studies in London, in a lecture in Washington D.C. in 2001, in which he argued that the terror war was the wrong term to use in what is really a struggle against an ideology, rather than a battle between states which has a clear beginning and end as in 1945.) What has happened is that America post 9/11, is now part of the global struggle against terrorism in a way that had not been the case before. Perhaps the *world* had not changed, but America did, and profoundly.

Now, over six years later, many in America are realizing that this is indeed the case. In the sixth anniversary edition of *Foreign Policy* magazine—the journal of the D.C.-based Carnegie Endowment—authors noted that while thousands had died outside the U.S. from post-9/11 terrorism, including the Australian tourists in Bali, the Madrid commuters in Spain, and their London equivalents on "7/7" (July 7, 2005), only *eight* people had died within the U.S. itself, a microscopic proportion of the thousands killed in the rest of the world. Although 9/11 was a seismic shock that should never be underestimated or forgotten, the actual damage done to the continental U.S. since that date has, in fact, been zero. Since that infamous day, America's centuries-old immunity from direct foreign attack has reverted to the norm.

Just take one example: airport security. Those of us aged thirty and above can remember the halcyon days when your friends or family could meet you from the plane exit, so relaxed was the security regime at the time. Such laxity has long since departed, and airplane lines can now be hours long, with the list of restricted items being changed, often arbitrarily it seems, depending on what the latest rumor suggests might be a dangerous substance to bring on board. Air travel, which used to be fun, is now a major obstacle race. (Palestinian and homegrown European terrorism necessitated a strict regime in European airports much earlier, but, having said that, nothing was ever as strict as such places are today.)

Consequently, according to sources with NATO links, it is unlikely that terrorists will try to use a plane for a terrorist attack, as they did on 9/11, precisely because security is now so draconian. In other words, the changes at airports since 2001 have worked, and have done so very successfully. (To take one example: Now that terrorists know that shoes are searched, another shoe bomber is most unlikely. The options for terrorists are diminishing all the time.) Not only that, but, as the U.S. Secretary for Homeland Security stated on the BBC in early 2007, American Muslims are very different from their equivalents in Europe. Most U.S. Muslims are middle-class, educated, and well integrated into their respective communities. They also tend to live with white fellow-middle-class Americans rather than in isolated ethnic/religious ghettoes.

In America and Beyond

In Europe, by contrast, there is a massive homegrown terrorism problem, as shown clearly by the events of July 7, 2005, when over fifty people were murdered in the terrorist attacks on London Transport. All of the suicide bombers were from good homes and professional backgrounds; one was a cricket enthusiast, while another was a pillar of the community who had been praised publicly and commended by the House of Commons for his work among needy schoolchildren. They were of foreign ancestry but with one exception, British-born.

At the time of writing, three people have been arrested in relation to 7/7, nearly two years after the actual events. A mix of ethnic and religious solidarity has made it well nigh impossible for the police to find others who were involved in the plots. The British government, thankfully, now realizes that prevention is better than cure, so is finally spending serious money on helping moderate Muslims engage with their own communities, thereby preventing (we hope) the alienation that causes so many young Muslim men from good homes and stable backgrounds to end up as radicalized, angry, extremist terrorists.

This is very much a European problem—not helped by hard-line American neoconservatives referring to "Eurabia," and postulating that an Islamic caliphate in Europe is just years down the line. In fact, since political correctness forbids such things as racial profiling of airline passengers from Europe to the U.S., one of the ironic effects of American right-wing paranoia about Europe and its Islamic minority has been to turn numerous white, Christian-descended Europeans against America, since the difficulty of even a simple journey to the U.S. by plane has now managed to annoy most of those brave or foolhardy enough to make the attempt.

But the main point is that the continental U.S. is safe, and that while in Europe there is a massive alienation and radicalization problem with the Muslim minority, the equivalent has not happened in America. To put it another way, the post-9/11 fear of many Americans has proved to be entirely groundless, since the security measures have, so far, worked well.

That is not to say that this couldn't change. One of the ablest Clinton advisers on foreign policy and terrorism, Steve Simon, now at the Council of Foreign Relations, has pointed out in his writing that complacency would be dangerous, and, so far as that goes, he is surely correct. As Irish Republican Army (IRA) terrorists once said, the government security forces have to get it right every time, whereas terrorists need do so only once, to achieve carnage of hideous proportions. So just because those who would harm Americans on their own soil have failed in the years since 9/11 does not mean that the U.S. has effortlessly regained its early immunity from outside attack. Evidence from British military sources (that Steve Simon would also have seen for his books and articles) suggests, for example, that containers are seldom searched when coming into port, especially those containing perishable foodstuffs that would become instantly uneatable if prematurely opened. However, although this would be obvious to terrorists seeking to take fissile material into an American port, the security services also know of the risks, and usually do far more to minimize them than they let on to the general public.

Consequently, much of the fear in which U.S. citizens live today is completely unwarranted, since those seeking to protect them are in fact, so far at least, doing an excellent job. The options open to terrorists have diminished, and breaking into Fortress America becomes harder by the day.

However, there remain plenty of people, not all of whom are enthusiastic and overt neoconservatives, who continue to paint a bleak and terrifying picture. Perhaps the most famous of these is the Harvard academic, Samuel Huntington, whose book *The Clash of Civilizations* has been a best-seller since it first appeared in 1996 (and in article form in *Foreign Affairs* in 1993), and which, according to many commentators and journalists, was vindicated fully on September 11, 2001. Some newspapers and journals even referred to 9/11 as the "Samuel Huntington moment," saying that everything he predicted had come to pass.

Huntington's theory is in fact quite complex. What he is seeking to do is to find an alternative paradigm to the post–Cold War era in which we live, or, as Colin Powell once famously observed, the post–post–Cold War days after the events of 9/11.

Back to the Cold War

In essence, the old Cold War bipolar conflict–the West, led by the U.S., and the communist bloc, led by the USSR–is now over. But rather than one power controlling everything–in effect, a now unrivaled America–there will be a new Cold War, not based on capitalist versus communist, but a whole plethora of groups based upon what Huntington calls "civilizations." These, in turn, are based not on economics but on culture, and, in particular, the most important part of cultural difference, religion. Huntington's theory of the next Cold War is predicated on the clash between these core new identities, or civilizations.

Huntington's main civilizations are based around the ancestral religions of the regions into which he divides the world. There is the West (Catholic and Protestant Christian), Eastern Europe / Russia (Orthodox), Islam, Confucian (essentially China, but also places such as Singapore), Buddhist (such as Thailand), Hindu (principally India), and Shinto (Japan). There is no Jewish civilization as such–one has to presume that Israel is, for all intents and purposes, part of the West–and there is also a difficulty in classifying Africa and Latin America, the latter, of course, being mainly Catholic.

To Huntington, future wars and conflict will be his *clash of civilizations,* a phrase he actually took from another writer, the great Princeton authority on Islamic history, Bernard Lewis, in a 1990 *Atlantic Monthly* article called "The Roots of Muslim Rage." But, that being so, it is true that everyone now uses the phrase in the sense in which Huntington made it infamous in his 1993 article, and 1996 book of that name.

In particular, the fact that Huntington feels that Islam has "bloody borders" and is the source of much of the civilizational conflict in the world today not only made his views notorious in the 1990s, but also enabled him and his supporters in 2001 to feel vindicated by 9/11, since the attackers of New York and Washington, D.C., were unquestionably Islamic and acting against the West according to their extreme interpretation of Islam.

But is it really all that simple? Are we right to be scared? More to the point, of whom should we be frightened, if, indeed, we should be frightened by anyone at all? Even as the first draft of this chapter was written, Christoper Catherwood was interviewed by a London radio station about yet another leaked British government report that outlined the dangers of homegrown terrorists, and the possibility that most of the people who are trying to kill us are not from overseas but are native-born fellow citizens, and thus highly difficult to detect through the normal channels of tightened immigration controls. *They don't need visas to come here—they are our neighbors, as British as we are . . .*

To understand what Huntington and the others trying to scare us are attempting to do, we first need to look at the history of the Cold War itself, since it is the aim of the fearmongers to create a new Cold War (and new terrors to go along with it) that is at the heart of what we are discussing in this book.

During the Cold War, life was essentially simple. In the so-called "romance of the Cold War," there were clearly good guys and bad guys, and there was no doubt whatsoever in the minds of most people living in the West that *our* guys were those in the white hats, and that the Soviets were the baddies in black, clearly in league with the Red Indians, who were also out to kill us.

To put this politically, there was the West, which believed in freedom, led by its superpower, the U.S., and the communist East, a totalitarian zone under the control of the other superpower, the Soviet Union, or USSR. Obviously, this is to simplify things somewhat; plenty of equally oppressive regimes existed under U.S. protection, from Zaire to Nicaragua (of whose leader Truman once remarked: Somoza might be a son of a bitch, but "at least he was our son of a bitch"). But Britain and its fellow Western European nations were liberal democracies, and that was not at all the case with those regimes occupied by Russian soldiers in the Soviet bloc.

Britain, not too far away from the Iron Curtain, took the Soviet presence for granted, and gratefully accepted the U.S. forces in Western Europe not as an army of occupation, but as a guarantor of safety from invasion. This is not to say that some didn't disagree strongly with such a perspective; for example, the Campaign for Nuclear Disarmament (CND) in the UK and the Green movement in Germany had very different perspectives. But dissent was a minority view, and when, for instance, in 1983 the Labor Party, under veteran CND activist Michael Foot, officially recommended taking Britain out of the NATO alliance, that party received the worst-ever defeat in its entire electoral history and was very nearly eliminated from British politics altogether.

In America, thousands of miles away, it was different. American children had to regularly undertake school drills against nuclear attack, so intense was the fear in the U.S. that World War III might happen, and that nuclear holocaust would be unleashed.

However, the Sir Harry Hinsley thesis—that of the former World War II Bletchley Park decoder and subsequent official historian of British Intelligence—proved to be more accurate than the terrors of many concerned American citizens. In contrast to the alarmists and fearmongers of the CND and the Pentagon, Hinsley argued that since both sides were armed to the teeth with nuclear weapons, and since nuclear war could not be won (such a conflict, if begun, would so pollute the atmosphere that no human, animal, or plant life would or could survive), the two superpowers would not unleash their arsenals and end the world.

We do know, thanks to pioneering academics such as John Lewis Gaddis, in his works on the Cold War, and from Soviet defectors to the West, such as Oleg Gordievsky, that some leaders in the Kremlin were occasionally crazy enough to contemplate war. But we now also know, since the Cold War is over, that while there were certainly some nasty moments (such as the creation of the Berlin Wall and the even more close-run Cuban Missile Crisis), nuclear holocaust did *not* happen. Deterrence, in other words, did what it should have done—deterred both sides from war—and it actually worked. Countless American schoolchildren hid under their desks back in the 1950s and '60s for nothing—not that a desk could have ever protected anyone from nuclear radiation anyway!

Then in 1989 the countries of Central Europe liberated themselves from the Soviet yoke and, with the exception of Romania, did so peacefully, without World War III ever taking place. Come 1991, the USSR itself ceased to exist, and the Cold War was definitely over. The world could breathe again—or so a few people foolishly thought. In fact, with the threat of nuclear Armageddon gone (the suitably named Mutually Assured Destruction, or MAD), the world became a *more* dangerous place, just as the late Sir Harry Hinsley suggested. Wars now broke out everywhere, from Kuwait to Kosovo, and with large-scale massacres from Bosnia to Rwanda and beyond.

There was, however, a major and very important difference: During the Cold War, many of the *local* conflicts were in fact superpower wars fought in proxy form, between various clients of the two major states, the U.S. and the USSR. Therefore, what was purely local—say, in Vietnam or in Ethiopia—became automatically part of the much bigger global struggle for superpower preeminence. Once the Cold War was over, local conflicts became just that and no more—*local* affairs with no ramifications outside of the areas in which the wars were being fought.

Think how different the war to liberate Kuwait in 1991, or the hideous Bosnian conflict of 1992–1995, would have been if there had still been the "bipolar" world of the Cold War, just to take two examples. The U.S. involvement in Somalia—at one time a Soviet client state—would have been impossible, certainly in the form that it took. The danger that mayhem in, say, the Balkans or Central Africa could trigger nuclear war—as might have been the case if diplomacy in the Middle East in 1967 had gone differently, for example—now ceased to be the case. This is no consolation to the hundreds of thousands of innocent civilians so cruelly slaughtered in Bosnia or Rwanda, but it does mean that for those of us living in the West, the terrible threat of being wiped out in a superpower nuclear exchange is something that we need no longer fear.

So for people living in what diplomats and specialists called "Failed States," the chances of death are now much higher, since war in such places no longer has a wider linkage of the kind that existed pre-1991. Here, fear, ethnic rivalry, and nationalist hatred are all closely linked, as the wars in the Balkans fought during the 1990s show only too well.

The Case of the Balkan States

Here we can have a brief diversion. Although this book is about the U.S. and fear, we can, in looking at the tragic events of the Balkan wars, see how fear was used to very considerable effect, especially by the Serb leader Slobodan Milosevic, to create such a climate that war and the committing of the vilest of atrocities became almost commonplace. Worse still, they were carried out by people on their neighbors: old school friends, work colleagues—upon those whom the perpetrators had known all their lives.

Academics such as Michael Hecht, and television pundits such as Michael Ignatieff, have written helpfully, in different ways, on these issues, and specifically about how fear was very much a factor in the massacres that took place. Ignatieff recounted the story of when he was under bombardment during the Bosnian war. The two sides—Serb on the one hand, Bosniak/Muslim on the other—were shelling each other, with terrible casualties on both sides. But in between the shell bursts, the protagonists would talk on the phone, reminiscing about the good old days, about mutual teachers, girlfriends, and colleagues. The truly awful thing about the Bosnian carnage was that the perpetrators had been raised in the same villages, gone to the same schools, shared workplaces, and much more besides. This war was not a case of Yankees from Maine killing Southern boys from Georgia; these were neighbors slaughtering neighbors. This makes it far worse, and one imagines that it was the same for the hideous bloodbath in Rwanda, in which Hutus, raised in the same village or neighborhood as the Tutsis they butchered—usually with no more than machetes—similarly committed genocide against childhood friends rather than against anonymous and distant strangers.

Ignatieff was right to call the Balkan situation "Hobbesian" in his book, *Blood and Belonging*. Hobbes, as Ignatieff is correct to point out, would have understood Yugoslavia. This is because the English Civil War, through which Hobbes was forced to live and which he was lucky enough to survive, was butchery of a similar kind. During that terrible seventeenth-century conflict, many a family was divided, with one brother fighting for King Charles I and another for Cromwell and the Parliamentarians.

How could people do it? This was a question often asked at the time, and for which, even today, years later, there are not always answers. One can disagree with Ignatieff and those who ignore the religious component of all that savagery. Other writers, such as Tim Judah and Paul Mojzes, are far more on the money when they attribute specifically *religious* differences as actually being pivotal to the whole conflict. *Ethnically* speaking, and *linguistically*, the three groups—Serb, Croat, and Bosnian Muslims—are, for all intents and purposes, exactly the same race, speaking virtually an identical language, as Noel Malcolm, John Fine, and other experts remind us in much detail. What makes them *different*, and thus willing to wipe one another out, are their *religious* differences. The Serbs are Orthodox, the Croats Catholic, and the Bosniaks are those Bosnians whose ancestors converted to Islam centuries ago, in the fourteenth to sixteenth centuries.

Ignatieff is right to quote Freud and that sage's famous phrase, *the narcissism of minor differences*; religious differences did not really matter for most of Balkan history, and it is in comparatively recent times that it became a source of genocide-oriented conflict. But several authors, such as Michael Hecht, have had a good go at explaining what to us, in the West, seems barbaric, medieval, and incomprehensible—forgetting, in our often-arrogant Western way that the Nazis and the Holocaust were committed by Westerners and within the lifetime of many who are alive today. Hecht gives a fascinating example of how people can be forced into actions that would otherwise be inconceivable for themselves, let alone others. A Serb death squad, say the Tigers, led by Arkan (now dead), enter a village and slaughter all the Bosnian Muslim inhabitants. They tell the local Serbs:

> *The Bosniaks in the next-door village will want revenge. You are the nearest Serbs, and if we don't protect you, they will surely kill you. For us to protect you, our price is that you have to do as we tell you—and that means helping us to find all the local Bosnian Muslims and help us to kill them. If you don't, you are on your own . . .*

If one reads accounts of various massacres in the Balkans—such as those described by Tim Judah in his books on, for example, the Srebrenica slaughter, when Serbs wiped out over eight thousand innocent Bosnian Muslim civilians—one sees how the local Serb men were compelled to become complicit in the atrocities, so that they would be guilty accomplices and thus under the power of the death squads. People who had lived in peace with neighbors of other faiths suddenly became butchers overnight, and, in tragically many a case, not because of innate genocidal tendencies, but out of raw fear that if they did not take part, they too would be killed. Fear is the key to much of the slaughter of recent years, and the

Balkans are proof of how ordinary, hitherto decent people can find themselves involved in such a level of terror that they will either do unspeakable things or at least tolerate, or claim to understand, those who do.

And the Holocaust...

One of the classic examples of this was, of course, German complicity in the Holocaust, and countless books about this have been written, many, such as Daniel Goldhagen's *Hitler's Willing Executioners*, highly controversial. One must surely agree with those British Jewish critics of Goldhagen who feel that to single out the Germans is in fact to let many other European nationalities off the hook.

The active, if not to say enthusiastic, involvement of thousands of Ukrainians as concentration camp guards is well established. Every single occupied country provided numerous collaborators, not just with the Germans but also with the Final Solution, even if the extent of that complicity was suppressed for many years, as was the case in France. Even British people cannot claim to be pure: Although the United Kingdom proper was never occupied, the Channel Islands were, and there, the local British inhabitants collaborated every bit as much as similar nationalities under German rule over on the Continent.

In Yugoslavia, such was the level of slaughter by the Croat collaborators, the Ustase, that it shocked even hard-bitten German troops as they witnessed the scale and sheer venom of Ustase atrocities. In other words, the Germans were certainly very guilty—there Goldhagen is correct—but then, so too were peoples all over Europe. German guilt is real, but far from unique. At the core of this was fear.

SEVEN

Who Hates Us and Why?

Oderint dum metuant, translated
"let them hate as long as they fear."
–Lucius Accius Telephus, Roman poet 170–86 B.C.

WHY DO THEY HATE US?

In this section, we will look at the Patriot Act and the American reaction to 9/11. For if, as has been suggested, radical, *salafi-yya* Muslims, following the teachings of Sayyid Qutb (and before him, of al-Wahhab, and before *him,* of Ibn Taymiyya) are really after control of the Islamic world—what they call the *Near Enemy,* as opposed to the West, or the *Far Enemy*—then we are in reality almost incidental to the *main* struggle, the control of the *Dar al-Islam* itself.

Back in 2005, Britain had its 7/7. Thankfully, the response of the British government was calm and measured—although whether it would have been had the terrorists succeeded in killing hundreds of people is an interesting, if moot, point. They carefully did not use the term "war on terror," a phrase that we saw elsewhere was rightly condemned by experts such as professor Sir Michael Howard as being wildly inaccurate. They were also anxious to emphasize that although the perpetrators were Muslim, this was not an Islamic attack per se on the United Kingdom, since the vast majority of British Muslims were, as the BBC's security correspondent pointed out, aghast at such activities.

The week after the near-miss atrocities, a British left-wing political magazine, the *New Statesman*, published an article on how much better integrated Muslims are in the United States than they are in Britain, and for that matter, the rest of Europe. (One of Christopher Catherwood's most fascinating off-the-record meetings in 2006 was with a senior British officer, a puzzled top Scandinavian diplomat, and a British Muslim judge, just after the riots in Britain and Denmark over the publication by a Danish magazine of what were, to any pious Muslim, blasphemous cartoons of the Prophet Muhammad. The sheer lack of understanding of any kind of religious perspective by the diplomat—mirrored in the response of many opinion makers and government officials throughout Europe—shows the complete gulf in understanding that exists between even the most moderate of Muslims, such as the judge we met, and the current leaders of what is now the very secular mindset of Western Europe.)

But in the U.S., as the *New Statesman* (and numerous other articles on American Muslims) has pointed out, the situation is very different indeed. In particular, since that magazine is firmly positioned on the political anti-American left, and no friend of George Bush, its main tenet—that Gordon Brown and Britain have a lot to learn from how America has absorbed its Muslim population, and that Bush has done far more than any European politician to help Muslims feel accepted as an integral, full part of Western society, despite his attack on Iraq—is one that is truly extraordinary. For a viscerally anti-Bush magazine to actually praise him shows that even the most hardened Bush-haters in Europe realize the significance of his encouragement of Muslim-American integration.

Furthermore, the article, by its U.S. editor, Andrew Stephens—no friend of the Republicans—went on to quote the fascinating recent findings by the politically neutral Pew Forum on Religion, which showed that 80 percent and more of American Muslims strongly oppose violence of any kind. This figure is far higher, for instance, than comparable statistics in Britain, where a scarily large percentage of British Muslims feel alienated and thus sympathetic to violence by their coreligionists.

In other words, American Muslims are *not* a threat; like Americans of German ancestry in World War I, or those of Japanese descent in World War II, they are no enemy to be feared within, but rather, patriotic citizens like anyone else who are therefore puzzled as to how on earth any of their fellow Americans could ever suspect them. How many terrorist cells have been found in Dearborn, which has a large percentage of Muslim-Americans? None at all, and indeed, since 9/11, not a single act of major terrorism has been committed in the U.S. Nor, unlike Britain's 7/7 bombers, who were British-born, have *any* Muslim-Americans taken part in atrocities either home or abroad, as we shall see. Most European countries, Britain included, where Muslim alienation is a major problem, would love to have the kind of peaceful, law-abiding Muslim minority represented by American Muslims.

This is why it is so astonishing that the U.S. has a piece of legislation as draconian and civil liberty–destroying as the USA Patriot Act. This act, well over a hundred pages long, is extremely arcane and very difficult to read at a single sitting (as we foolishly tried to do in order to write this book). Much of it is highly specialized and has to do with issues such as monitoring terrorist activity, banking, and, to be fair, affirmations that Arab-Americans, Muslim-Americans, and, for that matter, Sikh-Americans, are all good patriots who need their rights affirmed as much as anyone else. Nonetheless, the act represents a major intrusion of the state into the civil liberties of all U.S. citizens, and gives the administration investigating powers that it never had before.

One interesting provision, for example, says that if someone reports you to the authorities, the latter can close down your bank account without telling you or without giving you any reason for doing so. In theory, this is a good move against terrorists—one is hardly likely to say, "Excuse me, Mr. Atta, but as you are about to attack the World Trade Center with funds you have wired from Saudi Arabia, we will be shutting down your bank account!" The real problem with this legislation is what it allows *in principle*, and how it exploits ordinary Americans' fear of terrorist attack, giving the government powers over its law-abiding citizens that no one would ever concede in any other kind of circumstances.

Take the example just given: While one naturally presumes that the actual use of the new clause would indeed only be used against terrorists—say, in wiring money from overseas to commit an offense in the U.S.—nonetheless, the authorities now have that power, in theory, *under any circumstances*, and not just in order to do something with which we would all agree, namely to defeat terrorism and make such acts hard to carry out.

In Britain, one of the major problems, as discovered on July 7, 2005, is that the terrorists were *homegrown*. Since at the time of this writing in mid 2007, no prosecutions have been made or sentences imposed for the 2007 terrorist plotters who are charged with explosions in Scotland (under British law, caution must be employed when discussing this case), it is hard to generalize about those potential perpetrators, except to say that those under suspicion were not in this case locals, but immigrants who came to the United Kingdom ostensibly to work, and to take much-needed posts in the National Health Service, which is notoriously short of British-born qualified doctors.

But either way, these people would have had British bank accounts, into which their British salaries would have been deposited, and, given the equipment used by the successful 7/7 suicide bombers, the unsuccessful and now-convicted July 21, 2005, bombers, and the arrested but not-yet-convicted 2007 would-be bombers, none of these needed special funds that would have raised any eyebrows with the authorities, or indeed, probably anyone else. Extra bank vigilance from suspicious countries, such as Saudi Arabia (or, in the case of many Islamic extremists, in Pakistan), would probably be very useful, but the right to look at *every* citizen's bank account, without any judicial safeguard (which would not have to be revealed to the person who held the account) is the thin end of the wedge, or, to use another metaphor, the top of a *very* slippery slope.

Initially, this seems odd, but again, there is a very good reason that has nothing to do with whether or not the average librarian is a brave upholder of the free rights and liberties of American citizens. Under the Patriot Act, enormous amounts of normally private material can be demanded by the state—all your e-mails, for example, however confidential or personal. One of the things that they can insist upon seeing is all of the library books that you have borrowed; they can note, for example, that one of this book's authors has borrowed lots of books on Islam from the Boatwright Library of the University of Richmond (ironically, to write two books for evangelical publishers, as well as two other books on Middle Eastern history for mainstream U.S. publishing houses).

In other words, there can be quite innocent reasons for wanting to see a book. Surely the puzzled citizens of Greeley in Colorado might, for instance, have read many a book on the origins of extremist Islam because it was there, in the 1940s, that a hitherto obscure Egyptian schoolteacher, Sayyid Qutb, was so horrified at seeing men and women dance together at a very respectable church barn dance that he ended up turning to ultraradical and ultimately lethal extremist Islam, of the kind that led directly to 9/11.

So, to put it another way, is this all a sledgehammer to crack a nut? Not only that, but what if the wrong kind of government were to have the power that is granted to any administration under the powers of the Patriot Act?

And Back to a History of Fear

Neither author is among those (such as the otherwise excellent and usually fascinating bloggers, like Dave Lindorff for *CounterPunch*) who think that we are just a few steps away from an American equivalent of the Third Reich. In fact, such language is, to us at least, the mirror image of what is so wrong with the climate that the Patriot Act and the Bush government has created in the U.S. This book is about the creation of climates of fear by all sorts of groups—government, the media, big business—to advance their own private ends. But one of the things the blogosphere fails to do is examine things in their historical contexts, which is exactly what we are trying to do here. Toward this end, we ask: Have we been here before, and if so, how? Is the Bush administration uniquely guilty either within the context of U.S. history, or indeed, globally?

As we have seen, Democrat Woodrow Wilson was profoundly guilty of using the fear of German spies to do things very similar indeed to what Bush, Ashcroft, and others did after 9/11. The same applies further back, as we saw, to the Federalists using fear of the French to crush their domestic political rivals, Jefferson and his Republican Party. Republicans almost certainly allowed the odious Joseph McCarthy to get away with his lies for their own domestic political reasons; is it a coincidence that he was exposed as a fraud once they had safely regained the presidency after a twenty-year gap? Likewise, the hatred of the Bosnian Muslim minority stirred up by Slobodan Milosevic in Serbia is almost identical in kind to that used against the Jews—and with proportionately as horrific effects—by the Nazis in the 1930s.

What worries some about reading many blogs on the political left is that by using extreme language, they are creating their own climate of fear. George W. Bush might well be—and some would think, surely was—a disastrous president. Leading Republican politicians have come out as completely opposed to his failed policy in Iraq, and in fact, a cross-party consensus on this has now emerged. But is George Bush like Adolf Hitler? Come on!

The Danger of Parallels

However . . . as anyone watching many a fascinating video on You-Tube can see for themselves, many of the *principles* behind what the Bush administration is doing, precisely in the area of creating a climate of fear, *are* the same as what the Nazis were doing in relation to the Jews in the Third Reich. One must add that the stupidity of the Bush White House is not in the same league as the *55 million* who died as a result of Hitler's aggression between 1933 and 1945, including not just 6 million Jews, but also 20 million (and probably more) citizens of the Soviet Union.

Take the name of the act itself: the USA *Patriot* Act (the Uniting and Strengthening America by Providing Appropriate Tools Required to Intercept and Obstruct Terrorism Act). What does that imply about anyone who disagrees with it? Obviously, that they are not patriotic. As George W. Bush has said, you are either with us or you are against us (incidentally, thereby ignoring Christ's other clear words, that those who are not against us are for us). You are either with George W. Bush, or you are against America.

Here it is important to realize why historical context is vital. Bush is no different on this issue than Woodrow Wilson was in the early 1900s, or the Federalists were in the 1790s. From the point of view of defending the principles of civil liberties, justice, the rule of law, and all the other things for which Britain, the United States, and other Western democracies are supposed to stand, however dreadful the Patriot Act might be, *fear has been used, created, and manipulated by governments for hundreds of years.* George W. Bush is thus not unique; he is merely the latest, and his visceral Democratic opponents need to realize that unless we grasp this fact, we will actually make the situation *more* dangerous rather than less.

One day, Islamic extremism will go the way of Soviet communism and of twentieth-century fascism. There was a threat; it was serious; but it passed. But the point is this: *There will be a new threat*, probably of a kind we cannot yet envisage, just as no one could have predicted the rise of Al-Qaeda–style religious terrorism so soon after the end of the Cold War. But one thing we can predict: Governments, the media, business, small-town gossip, and peer pressure—all of these will exploit the new threat and do so for their own purposes.

So the departure of George W. Bush in 2009 (and we hope many of you will be reading this book after January of that year) will actually, in a real and very important sense, not make any actual difference at all. Fearmongering will not go away. It will simply take new forms and be a tool for those who would oppress and exploit us in different ways, for their own purposes. Currently it is the threat of extremist Islam, and the Patriot Act is the tool of a government that exploits fear of that horror in order to control the lives of its citizens. But another threat will come, and a successor to the Sedition Act of 1798, the Aliens Act of 1918, and the Patriot Act of 2001 will find its way onto the statute books. *Plus ça change, plus c'est la même chose . . . .*

EIGHT

And What About the Media?

With the press, it is safest to assume
that there is no "off the record."
—*Donald Rumsfeld*

THE AMERICAN FOUNDING FATHERS WERE ADAMANT ABOUT preserving the free press. Freedom of speech is perhaps a characteristic that uniquely separates the American version of democracy from other democratic nation-states. New technological innovations in mass-media communications, such as globally linked television broadcasting, the Internet, cell phones, and other emerging media have enabled Americans to express themselves in ways unimagined by the founding fathers. Fear is well understood by the media as a potent method of boosting ratings and associated revenues. In this sense, what we fail to realize is that sensational headlines tend to obscure rational debate.[91] Public spectacle is used to create fear as a means to reinstate a sense of common values or national sentiment. Americans arguably believe everything they see, read, and hear in the media almost without rational questioning. A good example is the great fear of tainted Halloween candy.

This exemplary story is one which still scares many Americans, despite its obvious mythical nature. In 1970, *The New York Times* ran an article with a specific example of potential tampering of treats and fruits during the Halloween holiday.[92] This was only one example of the media's attitude toward Halloween candy in the 1970s. The idea that children could be easily and untraceably poisoned by eating candy distributed by strangers was so widespread that by 1984, *The Washington Post* and ABC News reported that 65 percent of parents were indeed afraid of the poisoning threat. Despite the fact that actual evidence shows that only two confirmed cases of children's deaths being attributed to poison Halloween candy. In both cases it was determined that the murderers were the children's parents, not strangers seeking indiscriminant victims. The most sensationalized case in the media was Ronald Clark O'Bryan in Texas, who killed his son in 1974 with cyanide. In total fewer than several dozen children were poisoned by eating contaminated candy between 1954 and 2000; the myth of an unseen threat has furnished newspapers with something else on which to focus, thus creating a state of fear over what is an American tradition, one which should be a pleasurable experience.

Members of the media are not malicious individuals who sit in their offices and deliberately create fear. In some cases, the government uses the press as a willing conspirator to shape public opinion, as it did at the start of World War I when stories of atrocities were fed to the press as official government facts, only later to be revealed as mere propaganda. The American newspaper editors of that time were incensed at how easily they were duped.[93]

Newspapers and television stations will argue that their broadcasts do not shape public opinion, just as they claim violence and sex on television do not contribute to crime and sexual promiscuity.[94] Yet, growing up in the 1960s, one could leave your bicycle on the front lawn all day, and when Dad came home, he would remind you to put it in the garage; nowadays, it would probably disappear in thirty minutes. Was the past really that safe, or has the media portrayed the past in the present through two vastly different filters? Are we simply imagining a past where children played safely in the street because of a newly heightened awareness of numerous things we are told to fear, like terrorists, climate change, smoking, AIDS, drug addiction, identity theft, car accidents, and obesity?

To illustrate the point of how easily people are shaped by the media, one can merely look at a few events to realize that some people can be fooled by what they see. In 1957, at a time when postwar crisis was combined with a heightened desire for knowledge of other cultures, the BBC ran a program entitled *Panorama*, which featured a Swiss family enjoying its annual tradition of the spaghetti harvest. The documentary contained a series of frame images in which this family in the Swiss Alps was happily and melodically harvesting hundreds of (cooked) spaghetti strings from trees in their backyard. Many spectators, however, failed to realize that this was an April Fool's hoax, and they were indeed only too offended when they discovered, days later, that this documentary was false from beginning to end. Even though the broadcast was a not to be believed spoof on spaghetti harvesting, the BBC received hundreds of phone calls from viewers wanting to purchase spaghetti bushes. The moral of the story is that people believe the media—both broadcast and print—and consequently, the media has a serious responsibility toward its consumers.

The idea that the media uses fear as a sales strategy is not new. Although the media has control over its content, it's less easy to qualify how the public uses it. The huge number of articles written about the existence of weapons of mass destruction in Iraq, for example, while promoting fear of the unknown ("Does Iraq have the power to destroy us all?") also encouraged disbelief ("If they haven't found them by now, there aren't any"). The government, upset as always when topics of national security are brought into public view, seems to forget that the taxpayers are the ones who fund military operations. Freedom of the press, as well as human curiosity, comes attached to these matters, which have for so long been hammered into every American's mind.

In this sense, one can argue that over the past two centuries, a precarious relationship has developed between the press, the administration, the military, and special interest groups which, when viewed in the context of the news media's need to generate profits to remain a viable business entity, often blurs our perception of the objectivity of the press.[95] The military administrations cry foul when the press provides information on military activities during conflicts and, at the same time, the press cries foul when it appears that the military fed them information specifically to misinform potential enemies that might happen to be watching the broadcast. Government officials also actively use the press as a mechanism to manipulate public opinion and sway national attitudes on a wide range of issues by leaking information to the press.

The use of the media to manipulate public opinion is neither new nor limited to the United States. For example, in 1944 during World War II, Britain censored the press, instructing them to report on exploding gas mains rather than the impacts of V2 rockets. This is because Winston Churchill feared a panic would arise if the British people learned that the Germans possessed weapons technology that was demonstrably superior to that of the Allies.[96]

Another well-known example is Orson Welles's staged and updated dramatization of H. G. Wells's, *The War of the Worlds*.

On October 30, 1938, CBS Radio was broadcasting the music of Ramon Raquello and his orchestra live from the Meridian Room at the Park Plaza in New York City. Suddenly, a reporter from Intercontinental Radio News interrupted the broadcast to announce that astronomers had just detected enormous blue flames shooting up from the surface of Mars. The broadcast returned to the music of Raquello, but soon it was interrupted again with reports of how a strange meteor had fallen to earth, impacting violently on a farm near Grovers Mill, New Jersey. A reporter was soon on hand to describe the eerie scene around the meteor crater, and the broadcast now switched over to continuous coverage of this rapidly unfolding event.

Needless to say, the audience was terrified. Eventually, they were told that the meteor was not a meteor, but in fact, some kind of spaceship from which a tentacled Martian soon emerged, blasting the onlookers with a deadly heat-ray. Homes were evacuated and a state of martial law was declared. Original estimates depicted a reaction of total panic among 1 million of the 6 million listeners. Although this was later scaled down, hundreds of thousands of people thought the play was real, despite announcements before, during, and after the broadcast indicating that it was just a dramatization. People stocked up their cars with food and drove hundreds of miles to be with their loved ones.

People are more sophisticated today, less gullible, and less likely to panic. However, psy-op intelligence and technology has advanced to the point where a believable hoax of a hostile alien threat could be perpetrated again. The War of the Worlds broadcast was unlikely to have been a vast conspiracy to test the psychosomatic reaction of the American people to a hoaxed alien invasion. However, in hindsight, it proved to be a very useful case study.

Sometimes the administration is blindsided by the press, as was portrayed during the testimony of Donald Rumsfeld before the Senate and House Armed Services Committees (broadcast on CNN, May 7, 2004), where senior officials claimed to have seen photos of prisoner misconduct for the first time via a televised broadcast the day before. Ironically, when events such as the fall of the Berlin Wall or the Iraqi prisoner photos occur, no one questions the over-all investment in the intelligence community. Interestingly, during the same broadcast it was made evident that senior army officers admitted to having contacted CBS, asking to suppress the broad-cast on prisoner abuses in Iraq for two weeks. William Blum makes an important point on how governments take deliberate steps to use the press: "Propaganda is to a democracy what violence is to a dictatorship."[97] In this light, one could say that the media is to the terrorist what public relations campaigning is to the U.S. administration.

Another aspect to consider is how the use of fearmongering by the American press shapes the opinions of people outside the U.S., and perhaps even helps terrorists to recruit people into their ranks. For example, shortly after 9/11, columnist Ann Coulter advocated invading countries, killing the leadership, and converting people to Christianity, which later was used on the Islamic militant group Mujahideen Lashkar-e-Taiba's website, with the comments, "We told you so . . . the preparation for genocide of *all* Muslims has begun."[98] Terrorist groups look for good, solid, raw material to promote their campaign, and the American media provides them with a continuous stream of copy.

The failure of today's news media does not lie in their cover-age of events, or the reporting of facts; rather, it rests squarely on the lack of debate or a constructive dialogue to challenge the government to justify its actions. The long-term implications of the inherent failure of the media to maintain an independent view has yet to be fully understood in the context of the overall role of the media in the future.[99] If critical debate is totally eliminated, will the government be prone to ill-considered, poorly planned, corrupt, or disastrous actions?

The relationship between the media and its manipulation of public opinion needs to be considered from the perspective of how the issues that shape foreign policy and economic activity are identified, used, enhanced, and distributed to either promote or retard specific objectives or issues that rapidly achieve the status of public interest, such as McCarthyism, racism, terrorism, and, more recently, prisoner abuse. The central question is: Whose side is the press on? The answer is profitability, regardless of social impact or the long-term consequences of misshaping public opinion. There are three primary motives of today's media:

1) The media acts purely in its own self-interest.
2) The media panders to whatever administration is in power.
3) The media is a willing (although perhaps unwitting) partner in the promotion and legitimization of special interest causes.

Frankly speaking, fear and sensationalism are what the media wants; terrorist events are ready-made for television simply because they guarantee viewers. The media acts to legitimize whatever they report simply by broadcasting it, as noted by Neil Livingstone: "The media are the terrorist's best friends . . . the terrorist's act by itself is nothing; publicity is all."[100]

The Value of the News Media

Would terrorism be as effective if no one ever heard about it? If a car bomb in Baghdad killed three people and no one beyond the city hears about it, is it less effective as a political bargaining chip? According to Jean Baudrillard, "The media is part of the event itself, part of the terror, and its role plays in both directions."[101] This is not to say that the media is manufacturing the news as portrayed in the 1997 film *Wag the Dog*, however according to Stefanie Grupp: "the media creates insecurities where there were none before in the audience in order to sell itself. The news does not just create formats of fear because they are the adequate and justifiable frames through which a fact can be presented: the frame of fear triggers a heightened interest in a preconditioned audience of fearful viewers." One could argue that as terrorist organizations become more sophisticated in their use of the media to communicate their views, the overall return on investment in terrorism will continue to rise exponentially. Robert Kumamoto echoes this growing awareness of the effective use of the media by terrorist organizations:

> . . . *in a high-tech, information-orientated world, terrorists have discovered that the propaganda of their deeds will receive global attention, the value of which far outweighs the personal risks they assume. Simply put, terrorism, not nuclear weapons, provides more bang for the buck.*[102]

This brings forth another important question: Should the Bush administration look for terrorists taking courses at airline flight schools, or should they be looking in advanced mass-media classes at universities?

The media's portrayal of the common U.S. enemy is not restricted to the news outlets; Hollywood also plays an integral role in identifying enemies and/or amplifying the fears of the current social climate. During the 1950s and early '60s, World War II films painted a stereotypical portrait of Germans, while Westerns focused on prewar villains, the Native Americans. The late 1960s, '70s, and '80s made it clear that the USSR easily infiltrated Western society, moving effortlessly between national borders in every communist spy movie. The fall of the Berlin Wall and the dissolution of the Soviet Union left American filmmakers without an opposing evil faction; enter extraterrestrials, stage right. Hollywood quickly moved on to dissident factions such as terrorists, rogue agents within declining nation-states, and other disgruntled fundamentalist organizations to fill the void of an external threat.

Another aspect of the media is the exportation of U.S. movies and television shows that carry only the smallest hint of realism to foreign viewers who, somewhat naively, come to believe that the lives portrayed in these programs are an accurate depiction of the American lifestyle. One could argue that U.S. broadcasters in concert with U.S. product proliferation are exporting the right ingredients to trigger fear in their foreign customers—fear in the form of American cultural imperialism and the erosion of local cultural traditions, values, and beliefs.

The Department of Homeland Security uses the media to warn citizens of possible terrorist activities, such as the elevation to "orange alert" status during the 2003 holiday season. If indeed the objective of terrorists was to terrorize, it would be less likely that they would strike during times in which the government thinks they may strike. Consequently, the government could simply place the country on a continuous "red" alert; however, over time, it would lose its effectiveness, and people would be lulled into a false sense of security, only to be more surprised when terrorists eventually struck during the higher security awareness state.

Those of us who grew up in the 1960s had a fundamentally different relationship with television, newspaper, radio, and the men and women who reported the news. For the most part, news anchors were people of integrity. Reporters like Edward R. Murrow, Walter Cronkite, and David Brinkley, who came into our homes every evening, became part of the family, bringing with them one thing that is absent from today's media: trust. What was different was the way they reported the events of the day, in a context understandable to the average American—not embellished with personal opinion. Edward R. Murrow expressed well his views on fear:

> *We must not confuse dissent with disloyalty. We must remember always that accusation is not proof and that conviction depends upon evidence and due process of law. We will not walk in fear, one of another. We will not be driven by fear into an age of unreason, if we dig deep in our history and our doctrine, and remember that we are not descended from fearful men—not from men who feared to write, to speak, to associate and to defend causes that were, for the moment, unpopular.[103]*

Perhaps we wax nostalgic when looking back on the media reporters of the past, yet even in pre–World War II America, this emerging change in the media was beginning to be noticed, and held in contempt, by others in the news field, such as in Neil Mac-Neil's 1940 book, *Without Fear or Favor*:

On the whole, from the beginning of the Republic, the editors of the American newspapers have striven to give accurate and adequate information on the federal, state and municipal governments. They have been watchful for any usurpation of unauthorized power; they have been alert for evidence of graft or incompetence; and they have tried to keep the governments of the country informed on the opinion of the people. They have served as a link between the government and the people. Sad, indeed, is the newspaper and its editors who have not felt this sense of public responsibility. Newspapers must make money to live. It takes revenue, a lot of it these days, to operate a newspaper, but few newspapers work solely for dollars and cents. The publishers and editors feel that they are conducting an institution vital to the welfare of their community and nation; and they measure their success by the extent to which they discharge this obligation rather than by the auditor's report.[(104)]

Today, accurate and unbiased reporting of the news is the exception rather than the rule, and this is especially true in the television news media. News reporting has denigrated from journalism to soft news, or "infotainment," with media executives justifying their programming with glib sayings like, "We give the people what they want to see." David Morehouse, ex-U.S. Army Intelligence Support Command (INSCOM), said, "I found early on that you can't trust the network media in the United States to tell the truth. They're part of the problem, because they are owned by defense contractors for a reason—which is that the $900 billion global defense industry is going to control that which can sink them, so what do they do? They own the media."

As essential as media services are, it is likewise crucial that their power is used to inform rather than to scare, and that all those involved consider the ramifications of sensational news. Journalists like Paul Krugman have said that America needs a return to normalcy whereby the media divorces itself from the Bush doctrine of a world which is shopper-friendly surrounded by inspiring stories and war news.[(105)]

Considering the media's attitude toward an opposing view, which is seen time and time again in interviews on FOX news and others, brings forth a story from the 1956 book, *Empire of Fear*, about Andrei Vyshinsky (Soviet prosecutor general during the Great Purge) and John Foster Dulles (Eisenhower's secretary of state), who were discussing which of their countries accorded their citizens greater liberties:

> *Dulles claimed the prize for the United States. "Why, in my country," he said, "any citizen can take a plane to Washington and march up and down in front of the White House, shouting, 'Eisenhower is crazy!', and nobody will arrest him." Vyshinsky was unimpressed. "There's nothing remarkable in that," he retorted. "In the USSR also, any citizen can take a trip to Moscow, can go to Red Square and can march up and down outside the Kremlin, shouting, 'Eisenhower is crazy!', and nobody will interfere with him!"[(106)]*

Today, if a group of people assembled outside the White House and shouted "Bush is crazy!", the media coverage would simply turn off the audio and use the video clip with a commentator describing the scene as a pep rally for the president, or an antiwar protest or both. Having little or no oversight on the quality or accuracy of reporting the media acts to interpret events through a lens of whatever agenda they feel is in vogue. The bias in today's media reflects a growing imbalance in the power of politics, which has been legitimized by the fear of terrorism. One must remember, as Kavka said: "Political power is, to a substantial degree, a function of citizens' fears of one another and their beliefs about each others' attitude toward authorities."[107]

The freedom of the press in America is guaranteed by the Constitution; by contrast, a free press is something that must be achieved through journalistic excellence, which is only achieved through an independent, nonpartisan perspective. Unfortunately, the American people do not hold the news media accountable for the accuracy of their reporting, nor the impartiality of their broadcasts. Reminiscent of Richard Nixon's silent majority, which will not express its opinions publicly, today's television viewers are simply content with a staple diet of fear, terror, and sensationalism.

NINE

The Erosion of Liberty Values: Fear Is a Distorting Force

They that give up essential liberty to obtain a little
temporary safety deserve neither liberty nor safety.
—*Benjamin Franklin*

THE UNITED STATES' ECONOMIC DOMINANCE OVER THE LAST half of the twentieth century has led average American citizens to a level of social detachment from their global counterparts, what amounts to a cultural isolationism. This then fosters an American-centric ideal, that the U.S. definition of liberty elevates them to a position where they become sole administrators of a monopoly on freedom. Like capitalism, freedom takes many forms and adapts to the values and beliefs of indigenous cultures as a mechanism to facilitate a social harmony that is its most appealing quality. Unfortunately, the Bush doctrine has little allowance for the fact that each culture must be free to implement freedom within the confines of its own geopolitical boundaries, molding it into a version of liberty that best suits its population.

New legislation designed to thwart terrorism and money laundering sets in motion a process in which ordinary citizens will be engaged with increasing frequency in reporting on the actions of other citizens. For example, real estate agents have a new role during the purchase of the "American dream": If the agent suspects (even without any tangible proof, or only with proof that is subjective in nature) that a potential homebuyer may have obtained funds from questionable sources, he or she can contact the authorities, who shall in turn initiate swift actions. This seemingly isolated change in the social fabric of America raises several important questions, such as how can newly engaged real estate agents assess their buyers' source of funds? Are they qualified to do so? Are they legitimate representatives of the U.S. government?

The problem at hand is that by enabling and encouraging citizens to spy on the actions of other citizens, one recognizes one of the foundations of totalitarian states such as Nazi Germany and Soviet Russia. The mechanism of reporting on your fellow citizens can easily be misused by people employed in its action. For example, the net effect is that a person identified with a possible suspicious source of funds for a down payment on a house may have his or her bank accounts frozen until investigators determine if further investigations are warranted. During the time elapsed in the process of investigation, the individual's personal finances remain in disarray for what can become an indefinite period of time. One could argue that this delay would jeopardize most home purchase transactions. Therefore, one can speculate that this mechanism could be used by unscrupulous agents to retard certain people's ability to purchase a home for personal and private reasons—for example, to promote a racial agenda in a certain area of town, or other subjective attributes.

News anchor Keith Olbermann points out:

We have lived as if in a trance.

We have lived as people in fear.

And now—our rights and our freedoms in peril—we slowly awaken to learn that we have been afraid of the wrong thing.

Therefore, tonight have we truly become the inheritors of our American legacy?

For, on this first full day that the Military Commissions Act is in force, we now face what our ancestors faced, at other times of exaggerated crisis and melodramatic fear-mongering: A government more dangerous to our liberty, than is the enemy it claims to protect us from.[108]

Developing a Phantom Sense of Security: The Patriot Act

The world is governed more by appearances
than realities, so that it is fully as necessary to seem
to know something as to know it.
—*Daniel Webster*

How does the immediate reaction of the U.S. Congress to the creation of the U.S. Patriot Act serve as evidence for the link between fear, reduction of freedom, and the behavior of the U.S. nation when confronted with the enemy from outside? Freedom is compromised when legislators overreact and pander to the emotional distress of citizens by passing legislation such as the USA Patriot Act, which is poised to usher in a new-age version of McCarthyism. The implementation of the Patriot Act relies on two pillars of actions: sweeping new powers for law enforcement agencies to conduct surveillance; and the speculative powers of ordinary citizens (lacking any qualifications or tools) to "report on" the behaviors of other citizens based solely on suspicion that is void of substantive proof or probable cause. In May 1940, Franklin D. Roosevelt authorized the attorney general to secure information through the use of listening devices on persons suspected of subversive activities.[109] These new powers, which were granted under the label of "national defense," set in motion a process of surveillance during the postwar period that was to eventually fuel McCarthyism.

Reminiscent of the search for communists, whenever a society singles out a specific ethnic or social group and creates a condition in which that group is placed under greater scrutiny than the majority, the value of freedom is irrevocably eroded. That said, this legislation alters the balance between freedom and security in three ways: 1) by creating a condition of pseudoisolationism and thus keeping the American people at arm's length from engaging in worldwide issues; 2) by significantly retarding immigration as a mechanism to weed out potential dissidents; and 3) by reinforcing the objectives of terrorism by wearing away the attributes of freedom.

The development of more-stringent requirements for entry will not deter terrorists; rather, it will only reduce freedom and inconvenience law-abiding citizens. Terrorists who are trained to evade detection will continue to escalate their efforts as the barriers to prevent entry increase. Analogous to the weapons buildup during the Cold War, the new restrictions will simply act as a catalyst for terrorists to become even more invisible, while at the same time silently eroding freedom for all by permanently instilling a sense of fear in the population. Immigration is the foundation of economic growth, as it fosters the cultural diversity that is the cornerstone for a heterogeneous society, which does not simply extol the act of being free, but exemplifies freedom. Actions by lawmakers, such as reforming the student visa program and visa overstays, which are at the heart of the new legislation, is simply good public policy and should not have to be linked to changes instituted because of terrorism. The need for these reforms identifies the lack of a proactive comprehensive national policy because it changes only after catastrophic events generate enough momentum to initiate reforms.

U.S. organizations have demonstrated an inability to provide the necessary social-economic infrastructure, necessary to integrate nations that have undergone a transference of power, into a framework which encourages economic development. This development would, in turn, deter political corruption and facilitate integration into a global marketplace.

Modern Medieval Barricades

Constructing an impenetrable wall of legislation and government security agencies is analogous to erecting medieval walls around a city, or the trench warfare of the early twentieth century; it is clearly a dated technique easily circumvented by technology, as revealed by history. With the advent of technologies such as the Internet, Americans view this advance in telecommunications not as a mechanism to engage global cultures but rather as a medium to spread Western socioeconomic values. However, citizens in other countries are not obliged to subscribe to American values, by buying a hamburger, listening to American music, or watching movies produced in Hollywood. People in all cultures also have freedom to either incorporate or reject Western ideals into their lifestyles.

This is the fallacy of the terrorist argument regarding the spread of Western culture: It is a revolution occurring within the local population, and not an expressed intent to circumvent traditional sources of political or religious power. Hence, it is easier to attack an external enemy such as the United States, as the icon for intolerance, than it is to deter local populations into strict adherence to a cultural or religious dogma. The influence of technology on the behavior of society is evident, with a history of adoption and adaptation that spans centuries of technological innovation. Fighting the attraction of technological advance and its often-addictive effects is an exercise in futility. A proactive approach to the problem would be to work toward a balance of acceptable technological progress that permits a nation to actively participate on a level, global, economic playing field.

Foreign Relations in the Post-Saddam Era

Whosoever commands the sea commands the trade;
whosoever commands the trade of the world commands the
riches of the world, and, consequently, the world itself.
—*Sir Walter Raleigh*

Idealism is fine, but as it approaches reality,
the cost becomes prohibitive.
—*William F. Buckley Jr.*

To the average American, the influence of any nation-state's domestic and foreign policies on the global economy instills a sense of intellectual dread, usually due to a preconceived notion that any macroeconomic discussion will be a cacophony of seemingly unrelated numbers strung together by an underlying political agenda. If we strip away the mathematical aspect of the interplay between the policies of nation-states and social-economic activity, we can begin to unravel the relationship between the actions of sovereign states through which they protect, defend, and make secure its citizenry, with the need to regulate economic activity to encourage and nurture long-term national wealth. This is not to say the topic of macroeconomics and the causal effects of any administration's policies are not an extremely complex subject; however, if we break down the topic into a framework of interlaced global economic activity, a topology of the subject emerges that will lend itself to compartmentalizing the issues into more easily understood components.

To reduce the complexity of the macroeconomic issues, we will break the subject into smaller parts and examine them individually before reassembling them into a larger context. To do this, we will place these issues into a simple business context, which is not meant to diminish the importance of the issues, but rather to avoid diving into a quagmire of statistics and figures.

Global consumers understand the intrinsic value of goods and services regardless of their point of origin relative to their local need. In all parts of the world, consumers have an uncanny ability to identify inferior products, shun overpriced goods, and weed out poor-performing companies. Just as true is the fact that the trade flows in an increasingly interconnected world are changing to reflect the corporate competencies found in each nation-state, resulting in a global rebalancing of worldwide resources. The U.S. is no longer at the epicenter, and evidence is emerging that other economic actors such as the European Union or China may eclipse—

or at least rival—the U.S. as a major military-economic power.[110] The fundamentals of consumerism, which we will use as a framework to codify the complexity of the relationships between policy and long-term economic consequences, are at the nexus of this topic. The central question is: What are the long- and short-term economic consequences of the sudden shift in U.S. foreign and domestic policies in the post-9/11 global economy? The goal of our discussion is to understand the extent to which the neoconservative policies set forth by the George W. Bush administration and the 108th Congress of the United States will have on future economic and commercial activities. Simply, are the policies adopted as a reaction to the 9/11 terrorist acts placing the U.S. economy at risk in the long term? More important, can any nation build and sustain long-term foreign policy objectives that are based on an ideology of Edmund Burke: "The only thing necessary for the triumph of Evil is for good men to do nothing"?

One could argue that the promise of the new century's optimism is that military might will be replaced by economic collaboration, and the evolution of a global international agenda to usher in the next stage of human development. In this context, one could continue to refine the argument that if economic activities will be the defining factors of the twenty-first century, then the actions of the current administration are in fact setting the stage for the beginnings of a war of economies. An economic conflict may be a long-term result of drastic changes in U.S. policy that trigger legislative, regulatory, and other economic actions that will ultimately pit nation against nation in a struggle for economic dominance.

As we will see in Part III, the relationship between America and the rest of the world has also changed dramatically as a result of the process of this internalization of fear.

Part III:
Internalizing Fear:
Venturing Down a Slippery Slope

Human history becomes more and more a race
between education and catastrophe.
—*H. G. Wells*

IT WOULD BE UNFAIR TO COMPARE GEORGE W. BUSH WITH CAIUS
Julius Caesar Octavianus, because the behaviors and actions of each
are dissimilar in nature. However, Bush, like Octavian, is bound to
a foreign policy that is imposed on him by the success of his nation
as an economic power. In 29 BC, Octavian's return to Rome from
his successful campaign in Egypt came with a new, profound fear of
all things Oriental.[111] To build support for his campaign, Octavian
used a rising sentiment among the Roman populace of mistrust of
the East by extolling himself as the champion of Roman ideals. In
the same way, President Bush, like other leaders throughout history, used the lack of knowledge of the average American to amplify
the message that all Muslims were to be feared.

Jeffrey Kaplan has approached the post-9/11 Islamophobia by
examining the sharp rise in hate crimes directed at Muslims, or at
those perceived to be Muslim. As we discussed earlier in this book,
Muslim culture and religion are not violent by nature or aimed
at fomenting violent feelings toward other religions. Nevertheless,

as Kaplan has shown, the American culture soon became infiltrated with feelings of hatred after the 9/11 attacks. Most of these
hate crimes took place during the nine weeks following the attacks
against the Twin Towers and the Pentagon, after which they fell
sharply. Kaplan attributed the abrupt drop in hate crimes to four
variables: 1) leadership in the form of effective intervention by the
U.S. president; 2) law enforcement intervention on the federal and
local levels; 3) grassroots outreach to Muslims by religious, civic,
and educational groups; and 4) moral ambiguity in the rapid dissolution of American consensus over the War on Terror following
the invasion of Iraq.[112]

So the irrational fear following 9/11 was short-lived for a number of reasons. Why then is the underlying fear still ruling our lives?
Not just in America, but all over the world, intensified security has
inconvenienced us, violated our privacy, and interfered with our
civil rights. After all, is America not the land of the free? Is the
price for our personal freedom and national security so high that
it can only be achieved by the reduction of liberty? The freedoms
that American citizens enjoy are not a birthright; rather, they are
a privilege granted by an underlying social contract manifested by
the U.S. Constitution, requiring constant vigilance in their preservation. How can freedom be maintained internally within a nation
and in relation to other sovereign states without compromising the
liberty, rights, and freedom of others?

The erosion of freedom and liberty was a main concern for
America's founding fathers. Has the legislation passed since 9/11
drastically altered the freedoms and liberty of Americans? And,
if so, what message does it send to people in other nation-states?
Do the changes in legislation, regulations, foreign/domestic policies, military spending, and other government reactions signal

the decline of American economic dominance? More important, is there a parallel that can be drawn between the decline of the British Empire when it reached its apex and became the de facto world's police force, and the role of the United States in the early years of the twenty-first century?

In 1957, during the height of McCarthyism, General Douglas MacArthur was critical of the government's use of fear:

Our government has kept us in a perpetual state of fear—kept us in a continuous stampede of patriotic fervor—with the cry of grave national emergency. Always there has been some terrible evil at home or some monstrous foreign power that was going to gobble us up if we did not blindly rally behind it . . .

Our intention is not to depict the U.S. as a warmongering nation for the sake of simply making war, although many conspiracy theorists would like to argue that point. The focus of our analysis is in understanding the redirection of military and security forces in a post–Cold War world, and what effect the lack of a quantifiable enemy has on the national psyche. Michael McGinnis and John T. Williams draw an insightful analogy of the U.S. and the Soviet Union as having the "sociopsychological phenomenon of codependence, a relationship between two individuals whose neuroses nicely complement each other in the sense that each individual's neurotic needs and desires are reinforced by the actions of the other."[113] A fundamental question needs to be explored and answered: Is terrorism acting as a substitute for an old enemy, and now, because of new fears, acting as catalyst to move government powers closer toward an Orwellian future?

It Is All a Ratings Game

Historically, presidential popularity rises and falls on the public's fears, both real and imagined. We have conditioned the public to respond to its fears in predictable ways. For example, people fear crime, yet they hesitate to sign off on vast increases in spending on local, state, and federal law enforcement agencies. However, when people fear external attacks on the nation, they can be easily persuaded to fund wars if they believe that a threat is imminent. During the 1993 attack on the World Trade Center, President Clinton assured the nation that the perpetrators would be brought to justice. The attack was viewed and referred to as "a criminal offense," and although an intense investigation followed, few were brought to justice. On the other hand, the attacks of 9/11 were categorized as the "initiation of a war" perpetrated on the United States by non-state actors. According to Elaine Tyler May, the distinction is clear:

> *By declaring war against terrorism immediately after the September 11 attacks, Bush became the leader of a nation at war. War, if it has widespread support, has always contributed to the popularity of presidents. Crime has done just the opposite. Declaring the attacks an act of war, rather than a crime, elevated Bush's stature and boosted his sagging popularity.* [114]

But why the distinction?

TEN

The Consequence of Fear and America's Decline from Within

> Those who expect to reap the blessings of freedom must,
> like men, undergo the fatigue of supporting it.
> —*Thomas Paine*

WHEN MILITARY MEN DO BAD THINGS, THEY SEEK REFUGE UNDER the claim that they were "just following orders." When politicians make poor or questionable judgments, they raise a cloak of rhetoric on national security or patriotism. Let us now turn to fear as an internal mechanism leading to the decline of the American nation-state. Left unchecked, widespread social fear acts as a debilitating force which will, over time, erode American ideals, values, economy, and military strength. We can consider fear as originating from two distinct sources: one that is *instinctive* (such as fire, large animals, and other natural dangers), and one that is *conditioned*, which is learned (such as fear of strangers, which children are taught before they reach school age). Here we are concerned with conditioned fear, which is a learned behavior, and its importance in the context of U.S. business and the formulation of foreign policy.

With frightening similarity in tone, the use of patriotism and the subsequent call to action by the Bush administration echoes the same rhetoric of fear used by Nazi leaders to manipulate the German people:

Voice or no voice, the people can always be brought to the bidding of the leaders. That is easy. All you have to do is to tell them they are being attacked, and denounce the pacifists for lack of patriotism and exposing the country to danger. It works the same in any country. (Hermann Goering at the Nuremberg Trials, April 18, 1946)

Of course, parallels between Bush and Hitler are to be discouraged; but the same inherent problem is present in both circumstances. The actions of the U.S. government directly influence the ways in which Americans engage in their daily activities. During the Cold War, schoolchildren were instructed to hide under their desks in the event of a nuclear attack or, if outside, to fall to the ground and seek shelter. Many Americans between the ages of forty and fifty will remember the promotional videos of "Duck and Cover" with Tommy the Turtle, and will smile at the naiveté of this approach to what could possibly have been a nuclear holocaust, one from which one could allegedly be protected by hiding under a desk. This procedure, instituted throughout the American education system regardless of its potential effectiveness in saving lives, did, however, create a condition in which children immediately reacted when civil defense sirens wailed. More important, it made parents and children cognizant of the imposing ever present threat of the nuclear war by the allegedly soulless "Red menace" of communism.

Today, this same approach is being used consciously and unconsciously by the government as a means to generate public awareness. The anthrax scare in 2000[115] clearly demonstrates the public reaction to fear stimuli, as millions started avoiding the postal system and rapidly turned to e-mail and the Internet as less-dangerous forms of communication.[116] We have yet to understand the long-term impact of these new sociogenic fears on the American psyche and social fabric of the nation. The broad definition of terrorism found in sections 411 and 802 of the Patriot Act[117] has the potential, if misused, to erode freedoms granted by the Constitution.

The preservation of freedom, which should be at the heart of foreign and domestic policy, is found not in the erection of deterrents, but in the understanding of the root causes of international social discourse which pose a threat. For example, terrorism, as a social and religious discourse, is offering a criticism of U.S. foreign policy which the U.S. government has yet to address, and that U.S. citizens have yet tried to understand. Terrorism has the explicit goal of altering the behavior of a target people by employing methods designed to destabilize the population's psyche, thereby creating and sustaining a state of fear. In effect, its aims are to reduce the attributes of freedom, such as travel, security, and the right to self-expression, dissension in the form of public debate, all highly valued by the local populace. The implicit goal of terrorism is to promote the terrorist's agenda, which can be described as economic, cultural, political, military, nationalistic, or spiritual, and which is the root cause of the terrorist act. Therefore, the detrimental effects of terrorism on freedom cannot be eliminated without an examination of the implicit goals of terrorism—not simply the material objective (to cause panic), but also the ideological element of the discourse of terrorism (a criticism of U.S. foreign policy).

The greater threat to the American ideal of freedom is not a breach of physical security by foreign enemies, but to compromise the American spirit of freedom from within a nation as a by-product of terrorism—and that is an example of global spreading of domestic fear. Manifesting itself as legislation driven by emotions, fear, and racial prejudice, the express goal of terrorism is made complete by the passage of seemingly defensive new laws post-9/11, such as the Patriot Act. U.S. president James Madison at the Virginia Convention of 1788 warns us of the vigilance we must have in safeguarding our freedom:

> *Since the general civilization of mankind, I believe there are more instances of the abridgement of freedom of the people, by gradual and silent encroachments of those in power, than by violent and sudden usurpations.* [118]

In Madison's view the great enemy of freedom is not found in a foreign threat but from a gradual erosion of liberty from within the nation by individuals whom establish policies that undermine the characteristics and attributes of a free state. We must avoid being driven by fear and strive to look beyond the immediate pain and sorrow of terrorist events in order to address the fundamental preservation of freedom and the reestablishment of domestic security. We have to ask ourselves what these conditions in the world are causing us to do as we continue to make tradeoffs between security and freedom.

It could be argued that the Kennedy administration used the fear of Russian dominance in space as a mechanism to divert the

American public's attention from the escalation of war in Vietnam, just as today, the new emerging enemy is global warming, the issue raised to focus our attention away from the Iraq War. The diversionary use of fear has also been used by the Bush administration's attempt at a misison to Mars to divert American attention from the War in Iraq while maintaining government spending levels. The use of fear as a means of diversion simply places the attention of taxpayers from the negative realities to a positive looking future state. Thus our attention is fully diverted from the real topic of international interdependence and how fear of terrorism acts to enforce a sense of economic isolationism at a time when the world needs greater cooperation. What is important to note is that unlike previous generations the twentieth century economy is evolving into a highly complex interdependent set of financial transactions that demands greater collaboration between nation states. The root of the emerging foreign-economic policy dilemma was articulated by prime minister Tony Blair in his speech at the Labor Party's annual conference in Blackpool on October 1, 2002:

> *The paradox of the modern world is this: We've never been more interdependent in our needs; and we've never been more individualist in our outlook. Globalization and technology open up vast new opportunities but also cause massive insecurity.*[119]

The massive insecurity that Blair refers to is the fear generated from outsourcing jobs, foreign imports, megastores causing the closure of small shops, and other domestic fears. However, there is another fear, that of erosion in the brand image of a nation as a supplier in the global marketplace.

Adopting the perspective of a consumer, the topic of the long-term effects on U.S. commercial interests from current domestic and foreign policies can be simplified and viewed in a context of how the U.S. participates in a global exchange of goods and services. The use of a consumer-centric view is not intended to devalue the importance of this issue; it does, however, provide a means through which the complexity of the subject can be discussed as component parts. Looking at China as an up-and-coming economic actor, one can see the possibility that in the not-so-distant-future, the U.S. will find rivals that parallel its military as well as financial power.[120]

American Consumerism and Fear

The twenty-first century was greeted with visions of a technologically led global brotherhood, complete with a robust "direct democracy" ushering in an era of "friction-free capitalism."[121] The optimism that greeted the dawn of the new millennium has rapidly faded in the post-9/11 socioeconomic climate. The utopian vision that military might will be replaced by economic collaboration and a technology-laden revolution, enabling the development of a global international agenda for equitable trade, has lost its appeal as nations struggle to promote domestic self-interests. The dream of a U.S. hegemony that could have been leveraged into ushering in the next stage of human and socioeconomic development is dead. Placing economic, military, and foreign policy issues within the context of how U.S. commercial interests will fare during the next one hundred years tempts us simply to project the action of the last few decades into a U.S.-centric economic future for the coming decades. At first glance, the current military, economic, and technological dominance of the U.S. masks several trends which, when examined individually, do not present an overwhelming threat to the U.S. place in global commerce. Nevertheless, when these issues are aggregated, they provide evidence for a prelude to what could become a continal erosion of U.S. commercial interests.

The combined economic shocks generated by the dot-com aftermath and post-9/11 world events lead us to argue that economic activities will be the defining factor of the twenty-first century. The actions of the current administration are in fact setting the stage for the beginnings of a war of economies. An economic conflict may be a long-term result of drastic changes in U.S. policy that trigger legislative, regulatory, and other economic actions—ultimately pitting nation against nation in a struggle for economic dominance, using the military simply as a means to promote U.S. self-interest at the exclusion of any external trading partners. The alienation of traditional and potential trading partners holds enduring implications for commercial activities and other international interactions, as noted by Stephen Brooks and William Wohlforth: "Unilateralism may produce results in the short term, but it is apt to reduce the pool of voluntary help from other countries that the United States can draw on down the road, and thus in the end to make life more difficult rather than less."[122] Although the following figure is an oversimplification of macroeconomic interactions, it identifies, from a consumer-centric perspective, three dynamic forces that transcend geopolitical boundaries: production, consumption, and regulation.

In the twenty-first-century version of Adam Smith's "invisible hand," global competition is a dynamic self-balancing process in which the capabilities of corporations operating within a nation-state act in concert with external corporate entities and governments to form a loosely regulated single world market designed

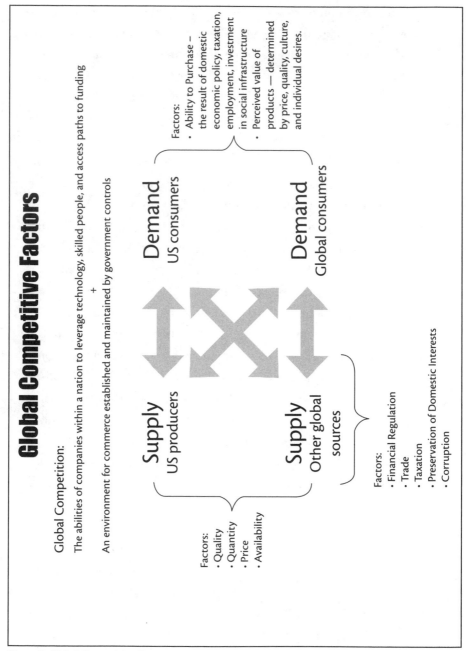

Figure 3. Global Competitive Factors.

for free enterprise. In this model, corporations acquire investment capital from sources inside and outside a nation to leverage available technology and skilled domestic people in order to create a value proposition for consumers in the form of a product or service. Consumers weigh a collection of factors, such as product quality, price, and availability to support, in turn, a purchase decision that is often based on personal motivational factors. Regardless of their motivations, consumer demand waxes and wanes due to two key consumption factors: the *ability to purchase*, which is the direct result of domestic economic policies, taxation, employment, and investment in social infrastructure; and a *perceived value* of the products offered by suppliers. For the most part, the latter is influenced by factors such as culture, gender, social preference, and individual desire.

The flow between supplier and consumer operates within a prenegotiated international environment for commerce, which has been labeled the *global marketplace*. Political factors such as the domestic and foreign policies of each participating nation-state regulate the flow of commercial activity and redefine the rules according to which buyers and sellers can exchange goods and services. Inside these complex networks of commercial interchange is an implied social contract between the nation-state, corporations, and the consumers who live, work, and operate within its national borders. The aim is to create an environment that enables an equitable exchange between parties. Unfortunately, with each nation-state striving to maximize its own self-interests, few national governments are examining the entire system of exchange holistically, toward a unified goal that increases living standards uniformly across all national borders. From a historical perspective, Brooks and Wohlforth note: "Great powers typically checked their ambitions and differed to others not because they wanted to but because they had to in order to win the cooperation they needed to survive and prosper."[123]

For one given corporation to have a successful product or service in the global marketplace, it must present to the consumer a proposition of value that can be easily understood and readily accepted under an unwritten contract of social trust. In this context, corporations presenting a product or service perceived as a good value for the money are automatically considered trustworthy by consumers, until they demonstrate a behavior that shatters consumers' confidence, such as the product being out of stock, its poor quality, or terrible customer service; these are all primary elements of the firm's value proposition. In order to appeal to customers and engage in commercial transactions, a company must rely on its value proposition as the foundation upon which its relationship with a customer is forged. It is in the context of a single global economy that every nation-state must also demonstrate a clear value proposition in order to engage the resources of a nation into transnational commercial activities.

One emerging role of national governments is to go beyond acting to promote domestic self-interest and facilitate an environment in which commerce can meet the demands of global consumers unfettered by hidden local agendas. Barbara Parker makes an important observation that is the nexus of the problem, stating that the more open the global economy becomes, the greater the reduction in national economic autonomy.[124] When national governments feel a loss of control over the import and export activities of a nation, this new dimension of trade can be interpreted as a threat to domestic economic parity.

ELEVEN

The Value Proposition of the United States

The key to making money in stocks
is not to get scared out of them.
—Peter Lynch

THE VALUE PROPOSITION OF ANY MANUFACTURED GOOD OR rendered customer service—regardless of the company that provides it, or the country in which it originates—is predicated on the consumer's belief in its perceived value. The cornerstone of capitalism is that consumers will seek out the best value for their money, and the competitive nature of business will always endeavor to reduce cost, improve quality, or increase availability in direct response to changes in demand. In recent times, technologies such as the Internet and eCommerce have revolutionized the potential for free trade by creating a condition for business where any company, regardless of size, can offer, deliver to, and service customers from any part of the world.

Liberalizing trade or international commerce argues that without restrictions such as import duties, export bounties, domestic production subsidies, trade quotas, or import licenses, each interdependent economic region centers its attention on what it can produce cheaply and efficiently, thus exchanging its products for goods and/or services that its economy happens to be less able to produce. The promise of advancing technology is to engage business in a new era of economic activity that is unbounded by the limitations of geography acting as a bridge between national cultures and local prosperity, as noted by Mozelle W. Thompson:

> . . . an "individual-friendly global marketplace" is one that has a foundation that places the consumer at the center of its "value proposition." In other words, it is a market that recognizes the importance of providing consumers with a basket of tools that provide consumers with a means to feel safe and confident to participate in the marketplace.[125]

Therefore, one can put forth the notion that in a global marketplace, U.S. goods and services must have a distinct value proposition to the consumers of the world in order to remain competitive. The elements of a value proposition can be codified into distinct components in which actions such as policies, treaties, regulations, and other economic instruments can be measured, as illustrated in the figure below.

Brand Image

In business, brands play an essential role in attracting customers to products. In today's global environment, brands are a double-edged sword that also attract the attention of special interest groups such as terrorists, anticapitalists, animal activists, environmentalists, and social activists. Americans who have traveled over the last twenty years are witnessing a fundamental change in the American brand

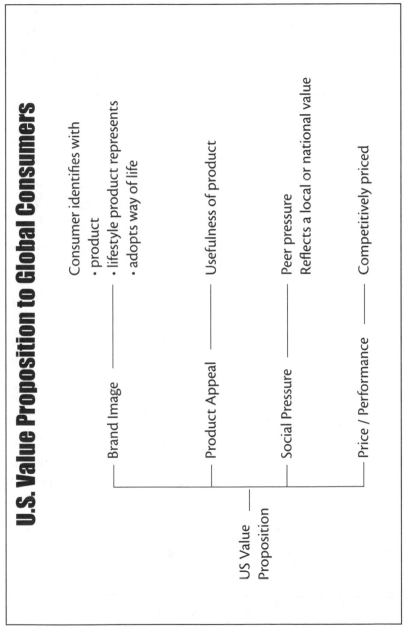

Figure 4. U.S. Value Proposition to Global Consumers.

identity in the eyes of global consumers. U.S.-based brands in the period between World War II and the mid-1980s were crafted simply as mechanisms to introduce new goods and services, promoting an identity of convenience, modernism, and prosperity made possible by ever-increasing waves of technological innovation.[126]

Since the 1980s, however, increased global and domestic competition have continually acted to commoditize goods and services, thus reducing prices and blurring product differentiators, resulting in a change of focus for U.S. brands, which now appeal to consumer attitudes like basic needs, intangible desires, and emotional wants. The individualization of consumer demand is not felt with equal vigor across the globe, being, in some cases, one component in a backlash against American products. For many people, brands act to define themselves as individuals by relating to a commercial or national identity,[127] replacing traditional mechanisms of self-realization such as joining a church, club, or political party; individual ideology; the consumer's workplace, hobbies, or community involvement; and other forms of social belonging.

In many cases, the symbolism of this individuality, coupled with American military power and economic dominance, serves as an icon for the processes of globalization and disintermediation. To date globalization has been characterized as a process of propagating the American culture to world markets. Disintermediation, on the other hand, has come to mean the use of advanced technology to eliminate intermediaries, thus propelling American goods and services to world markets bypassing domestic suppliers. Each factor has acted to broadcast an image of American goods, services, lifestyles, and cultures to consumers worldwide. This propagation of American culture establishes a fear of an erosion of local culture in the older generations, nationalists, and conservatives of other nations.

Culture and national identity are increasingly becoming elementary facets in generating consumer demand for goods and services. Mark Neal observes that cultural identity and national origin have long been a defining mechanism—both positively and negatively—for product and brand recognition. Positive examples include the engineering excellence of German cars; the excellent quality of French perfumes; and the elegance and status of Italian fashion. Negative examples include Russian cars, Polish shoes, German dresses, and Italian insurance policies.[128]

The U.S. brand is an aggregation of corporate logos that act not simply as a mechanism to attract global consumers to American products, but also as a means of communicating American ideals. Corporations such as McDonald's, Coca-Cola, and Ford are icons for capitalism, globalization, and the encroachment of technology into everyday life. In turn, these icons become a perceived threat to local lifestyles, beliefs, and values, providing special interest groups within any nation-state with a convenient target to vent societal anger in the form of violent acts or corporate boycotts. Corporate brands will be increasingly at risk as anticapitalist / anti-American organizations begin to use technologies such as the Internet to coordinate their objectives (in most cases, with a nonviolent approach). An organization such as Countercurrents.org, formed in March 2002, publishes a list of corporate brands and their associated products that are on their boycott list.[129]

Globalization as a source of fear is key because an external factor such as globalization is a manifestation (real or imagined) of fear of others. The process of globalization is intrusive to a local culture because of its often-conquering characteristic that imposes rules and aspects of their culture on a conquered population primarily to maintain order and propagate a more-homogenous social behavior. The economic inheritance of globalization is that economy, military power, social structures, and, to some extent, cultures and religions all endorse the expansion of a dominant country or ideology, such as "Americanization" during the twentieth century, British imperialism in the nineteenth century, French cultural dominance in the seventeenth and eighteenth centuries, and Spanish and Portuguese expansionism in the sixteenth century.

It can be argued that as economic activities across borders become more intertwined, they must adapt in order to become more synchronized in output and more aware of the economic environment in which they operate. The synchronization of commercial activity, trade, foreign investment, access routes to capital, and other economic measures over time will achieve a level of operational synergy, ultimately establishing a synergistic economy, or "synconomy."[(130)] However, synchronization and economic interdependence enabled by technological advances can be interpreted initially as a threat to traditional mechanisms of control. As Walter Wriston points out, the mechanisms of control are the perceived essence of the nation-state:

> *The mechanisms of control are being redefined as technology alters and reshapes the functions of the nation-state. An important point for the discussion on the brand image of the United States is that the process of globalization itself is undergoing a structural change. To oversimplify the process, it can be argued that in previous decades and centuries, globalization as a force was an external conquering power that directly changed the commerce, culture, and societal structure of a nation-state. Today, this external power is being replaced by an evolving process of progressive aware-*

ness within an interconnected global structure. Simply, as the ideals, values, and attributes of one society are more freely exchanged, the effects of globalization become localized by people who are electing, through their consumption and habits, to adopt or attain various aspects of cultures from other peoples.[131]

From the perspective of the U.S. brand identity—or perhaps the brand identity of any nation-state—this shifts globalization from an external process of cultural imposition to a process taking place within a nation-state by individuals who, by their own personal choice, are seeking to replicate that lifestyle, or the values of a distant culture. Multinational corporations are adapting their brands to this phenomenon by incorporating the relevant factors of culture to customize products and services, thereby delivering maximum appeal to significant market segments within specific geographies. This is seen in organizations like McDonald's, selling *aloo tikki* in Bombay, teriyaki burgers in Tokyo, flatbread McArabia in Amman, and kosher McNuggets in Tel Aviv.[132]

The combination of the emerging synconomy and the shift in the process of globalization presents a complex problem for the brand image of the U.S., because it can be perceived as an external threat for groups who prefer to preserve the national culture and local values. Moreover, the shift in globalization to an internal process is initiating a fundamental change within local societies that has fostered violent reactions from incumbent social organizations and special interest groups. Multinational corporations are now realizing that people have a greater awareness of world affairs, cultures, and beliefs, made possible by advances in telecommunication technologies, such as television and the Internet. As a result, corporate brands must change to reflect the changing global attitudes toward a perceived U.S. economic imperialism. Like corporations, foreign and domestic policy makers must realize that it is the commonality of culture that binds together contemporary societies that are not simply linked to a specific social behavior, such as religion, but to many social attributes that are intertwined to form an effective common culture.[133]

Therefore, to manage the brand image of the United States effectively, one must consider that the three dimensions of globalization (economic, cultural, and political) each present governments (like their corporate counterparts) with an additional set of variables to factor into national competitive strategies.[134] Even with the rising dissatisfaction with U.S. foreign policy, American brands have maintained a level of popularity across the globe, supported by multinational sales figures that testify to the effectiveness of their branding strategies. Until now, American product brands in many cases have remained unscathed by global events, although there have been isolated incidences indicating that the total volume of products, services, and cultural exports (like television, music, and media) is continuing to rise.

In contrast, most Americans are unable to envisage the indignation they trigger in other cultures that are the recipients of this continual, relentless stream of exported American multimedia programming. The average American is insulated from non-American cultural products, as described by Ziauddin Sardar and Merryl Wyn Davies: "The musical scene is almost as uniform as its televisual cousins—an unbroken vista of American pop, hip-hop, and country, broken only by the occasional breakthrough of a big British band."[135] One could argue that the first generation of telecommunication technologies (such as the Internet) was a process of projecting American ideals to all parts of a connected global community. More important, one can assert that the next generation of these technologies will be the rise of non-American cultural awareness, resulting from an ever-increasing volume of use by non-American users. Although English is the single most dominant language on the Internet—with 280 million English-speaking users in 2004, and projected to rise to 470 million by the end of 2007—statistics are projecting non-English European language use of the Internet to increase to 328 million, and Asian language use to skyrocket to 329 million users at the same period.[136]

Factors That Alter the Value Proposition

First, let us assume that the "cause and effect" relationship in economic cycles in most cases spans U.S. administrations. Policies set in motion during one administration often result in economic downturns or upturns that are in turn blamed or reaped by whichever administration is in power. However, catastrophic events such as 9/11 initiate an immediate and possibly hasty response, to be expected as a means of soothing the grief of the American people and reestablishing a sense of increased safety during turbulent times. One can argue that in the haste to craft reactive legislation, the resulting plethora of U.S. policy changes, fueled by the heightened rhetoric of danger, may have temporarily blinkered the process of placing foreign and domestic policy decisions that shape the long-term economics of the country into a proper global context.

On the surface, the rhetoric surrounding the Bush administration's view on terrorism infers that its foreign and domestic policies are now based on an eighteenth-century doctrine inherited from Christian morality, and expressed by Edmund Burke: "The only thing necessary for the triumph of evil is for good men to do nothing."[137] The shift from a reactive defensive posture to a more-aggressive preemptive offensive stance toward potential anti-terrorist actions is interpreted by world peoples as a fundamental disregard of a basic American ideal—one in which a person is innocent until proven guilty. Equally, one can argue that many aspects of today's neoconservative approaches are in direct response to a perceived overliberalization of trade during the 1980s and 1990s. Each attribute of the U.S. value proposition is, over time, experiencing both a direct and indirect erosion of value by neoconservative policies. The following figure illustrates how political perceptions outside the United States act in a similar way, as corporations often lose brand value in the eyes of customers.

A secondary effect of trade liberalization is its impact on local cultures in all parts of the world. Catherwood makes an important observation: "[I]dentity—nationalist, religious, cultural, and political—is at the heart of much of the conflict in the world today."[138] Cultural diversity is a rising factor in stimulating demand in a global economy. Newly forming commerce and banking channels are being developed to serve highly specialized needs in niche markets, such as the Islamic Banking Network,[139] which acts as a mechanism to educate individuals in the idiosyncrasies of Islamic banking; and Muslim-Investor.com, designed to open a dialogue between Islamic scholars and the customers of individual financial services.[140]

Why Is the U.S. Value Proposition Vital to Long-Term Economic Growth?

It can be argued that in the future, a larger percentage of U.S. domestic production will be increasingly interdependent on foreign

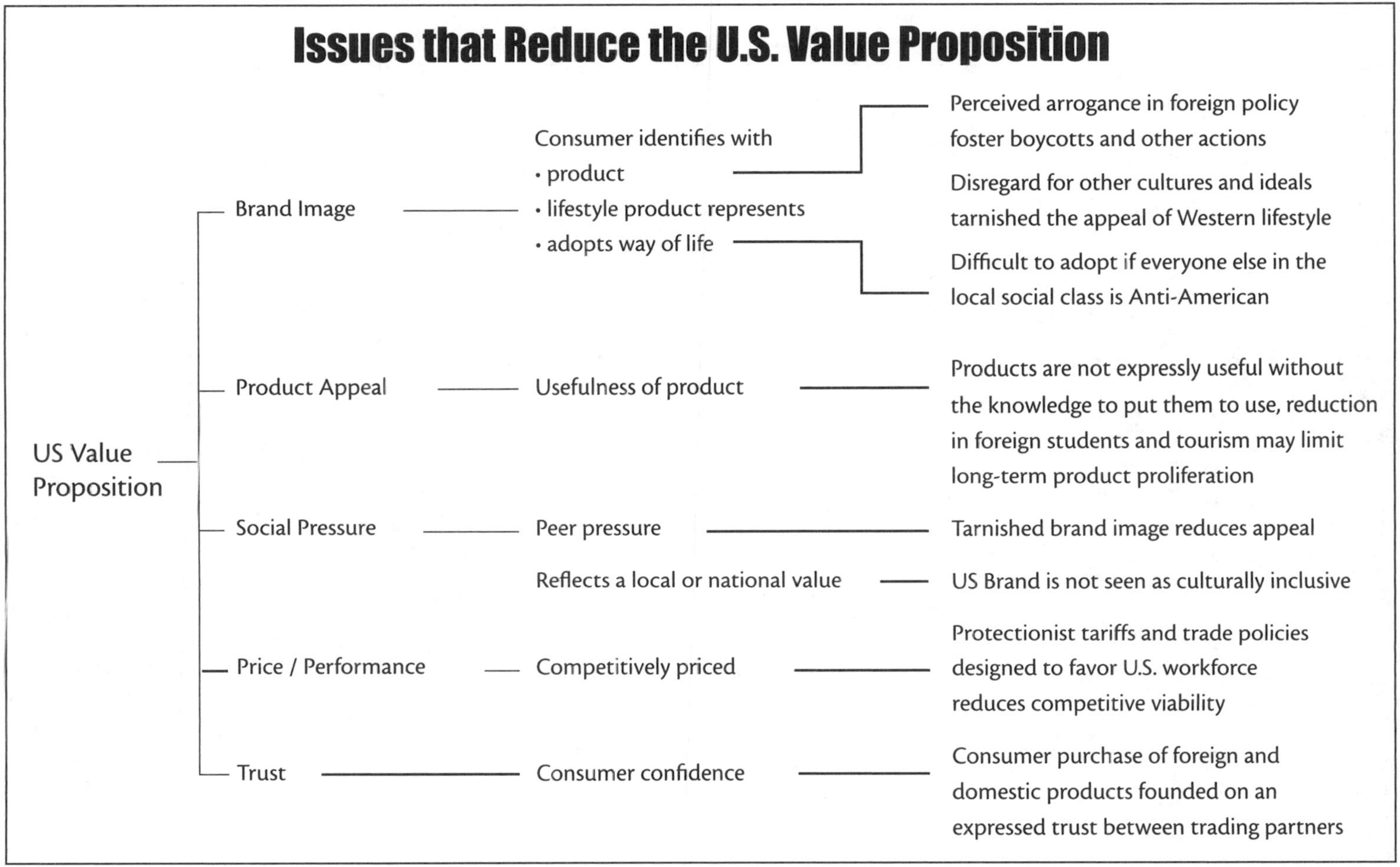

Issues that Reduce the U.S. Value Proposition

US Value Proposition

Brand Image — Consumer identifies with
- product
- lifestyle product represents
- adopts way of life

Perceived arrogance in foreign policy foster boycotts and other actions

Disregard for other cultures and ideals tarnished the appeal of Western lifestyle

Difficult to adopt if everyone else in the local social class is Anti-American

Product Appeal — Usefulness of product

Products are not expressly useful without the knowledge to put them to use, reduction in foreign students and tourism may limit long-term product proliferation

Social Pressure — Peer pressure

Tarnished brand image reduces appeal

Reflects a local or national value

US Brand is not seen as culturally inclusive

Price / Performance — Competitively priced

Protectionist tariffs and trade policies designed to favor U.S. workforce reduces competitive viability

Trust — Consumer confidence

Consumer purchase of foreign and domestic products founded on an expressed trust between trading partners

Figure 5. Issues that Reduce the U.S. Value Proposition.

consumers. This can be attributed to two key factors: First, as the U.S. baby-boom generation dies over the next twenty-five years, businesses can expect a drop in the overall consumption of durable goods, computers, and many other domestically produced goods and services. Second, as the U.S. market becomes saturated within specific industrial sectors, foreign markets will become the next logical source for growth.

Two additional factors rarely considered must be assessed when contemplating the U.S. value proposition in the context of long-term growth. First, that one can attribute a minority percentage of sustained production over the previous twenty-five years to the continual influx of immigrants; second, the increase in the rate of divorce. In the case of immigration, the vast majority of individuals have inherited a preconceived notion that immigrants arrive in a country penniless and destitute, looking for a handout. This view has it origins in the first half of the twentieth century, and no longer reflects the financial condition of early-twenty-first-century immigrants who are increasingly arriving with substantial bank accounts. John Micklethwait and Adrian Wooldridge have argued that immigration occurs in two distinct forms, categorized by social-economic means: despair and choice, the latter now overtaking the former.[141] Immigration, regardless of its motivations, provides the U.S. economy with a consistent demand for durable goods and other products as immigrants establish households. One can place the economic activity associated with divorce in the same light; when a couple or family unit is separated, it immediately generates the demand for an additional social infrastructure and goods. Simply, a newly divorced person—like an immigrant—must purchase durable goods and services to establish and maintain their existence.

If we consider these factors in the context of U.S. total economic output, we can see that there is a potential downturn in consumer spending which can only be countered by an increase in international trade, exports, and a higher degree of participation in a global economy. Therefore, it is a critical aspect of all foreign policy decisions to position the U.S. in the best competitive light.

In the short term, perhaps during the next decade, the U.S. will continue to be an economic powerhouse almost unrivaled in commercial activity. However, U.S. economic supremacy is not guaranteed, and may soon be rivaled by China's growing economic and military wherewithal.[142] One can make a clear case that in the long-term interest of economic stability, U.S. policies must take steps to avoid potential trade wars and negotiate a position of equality for American businesses in order to compete equitably in a global economy.

The flow of capital for direct investment in both foreign and domestic marketplaces is the key to transnational economic activity, because it provides a mechanism for corporations large and small to seek out funding sources to capitalize on opportunities as they materialize in a dynamic marketplace. However, since the fall of the Berlin Wall in 1989, the world is increasingly shaped by economic activities that are not attributed to governmental actions, but by the actions of the financial markets. Thomas Friedman characterizes this phenomenon as an "Electronic Herd" comprising two key actors: faceless stock, bond, and currency trades using globally networked computers to move money around from mutual funds to pension funds to emerging market funds; and multinational corporations spreading factories around the world, constantly shifting them to the most efficient, low-cost producers. In Friedman's view, the Electronic Herd thrives and grows as a direct result of the

democratizations of finance, technology, and information, virtually rivaling governments as the primary source of capital for both
companies and countries.[143]

One of the primary functions of government is to facilitate
trade, commerce, and finance, which are the key ingredients for
corporations to operate in a connected global economy. These
essential elements are integral for maintaining the value proposition of the United States, because as markets that were once limited
to one country or continent now merge into a single global market,
foreign and domestic policies must act as a catalyst for economic
growth and equitable trade. Technological connectivity, synchronization, engaged participation, and recognition as an equitable
trader are the hallmarks of new economic activities defining the
central issues of globalization.

TWELVE

Effects of U.S. Policies on the Value Proposition of Its Goods and Services

Fear is, I believe, a most effective tool in destroying the soul of an individual—and the soul of a people.
—*Anwar el-Sadat*

THE OVERARCHING THEME IN THE U.S. ECONOMIC MIND-SET is the steadfast belief that capitalism and democracy are linked in a symbiotic relationship that flourishes best under fair trading relationships with other nation-states. As the interdependence of economic activities between nation-states matures, there is a desire to develop ever-increasing liberalized trade relations to facilitate businesses' need to reach cheaper sources of goods and services and to create pathways to distant customers. Under a liberal approach to trade, a greater globalization of economic activity will occur first within multinational, transnational, and international corporations, followed by a rise in cross-border commerce within traditionally domestic companies, made possible by advancing commerce technologies.

Theoretically, the socioeconomic advances in the quality of life of any nation-state are directly proportional to increases in the inflow and outflow of goods and services operating in a free market. The erection of trade barriers and other domestically driven protectionist regulation, taxation, or tariffs retards the world's ability to embrace a capitalistic doctrine as a credible mechanism for social structure. A side effect of reactionary legislation such as the Patriot Act is the added cost to businesses associated with compliance, such as tracking terrorists and money laundering in the financial services industry, where the cost will be incorporated into the fees charged to depositors.[144] The underlying idea is that in a transparent economic environment, any bastion of capitalism, such as the United States, the European Union, or Japan, must set the example for how the next generation of global commerce will be conducted by all global actors.

A transparent economic environment is established when the motivations for trade (such as job preservation or investment needed to reeducate specific segments of the population and commercial activities) are discussed and addressed in an open forum. In this forum, nation-states negotiate for trade practices that benefit local people through a process of balancing global resources, much in the same way a multinational corporation adjusts its production capacity to react to changes in demand. In an intertwined global economy, two factors must be considered: the rate at which equitable trade practices can be adopted by all nations, versus the rate at which the U.S. regulates its openness to external trade partners. In the same way businesses forge international cooperative partnerships to achieve a balance between transnational economic activities, industrial and developing nations must agree on a fundamental set of operating guidelines, described by David Hume as: ". . . three fundamental rules of nature, that of stability of possession, of its transference by consent, and of the performance of promises."[(145)]

Without these operating guidelines, isolationism can occur when a nation intends to protect and defend its economic activities, as demonstrated by the influence of special interest groups on commercial activities, such as in the case of French farmers, or as a by-product of actions of other nation-states in retaliation to internal conditions, ideologies, or social unrest, such as in the U.S. embargo with Cuba. Under the rhetoric of making the world a safer place and protecting against terrorists, drug dealers, and others identified under a doctrine of "forces of evil," the United States is sending a clear message to all nations that the U.S. economy is the most important; all others are not relevant to the interest of the United States. However, as globalization continues, the U.S. economy becomes increasingly interdependent on international corporate and government cooperation. One factor to consider as a benefit to interdependency is that in a global economy, when an industry sector in a specific country (such as personal computer technology in the U.S.) reaches a saturation point, growth slows due to flattening of demand. Then the next generation of economic activity can only be found in the global marketplace. Other factors—such as the cross-border relationships that form within corporations and between corporations as a result of outsourcing, partnering, associations, and affiliations—are in direct response to domestic consumers' relentless desire to reduce the cost of production.

Participation in the global marketplace is predicated on an expressed trust between international governments, corporations, and consumers, and built on a compound set of relationships that over time act to lubricate economic activity. That said, the increasing dialogue on neoconservatives in the media, academic circles, and public opinion acts to reduce the credibility of the U.S. value proposition. The Bush administration's principal policy architects provide ample sound bites to turn global consumers away from U.S. products and services in the same way bad press and product recalls affect a corporation's ability to sell products. Often, even as a product is corrected, the stigma of previous problems or conditions lingers for years. The value proposition is inexorably damaged by rhetoric that can be interpreted as isolationist or preservationist, or conveys a disregard for the sovereignty of other nation-states while in the pursuit of U.S. national interests, such as this statement by Condoleezza Rice:

> *As a matter of common sense and self-defense, America will act against such emerging threats before they are fully formed . . . We must be prepared to stop rogue states and their terrorist clients before they are able to threaten or use weapons of mass destruction against the United States or our allies and friends.*[(146)]

This type of military/economic–based communication sends an all-too-familiar message to global citizens that still remember defining moments of the twentieth century, in words uttered by one of Europe's former leaders, as noted by Linda Heard:

> *We have no interest in oppressing other people. We are not moved by hatred against another nation. We bear no grudge. I know how grave a thing war is. I wanted to spare our people such an evil. It is not so much the country, it is*

rather its leader. He has led a reign of terror. He has hurled countless people into the profoundest misery. We have displayed a truly exemplary patience, but I am no longer willing to remain inactive while this madman ill-treats millions of human beings.[147]

Of course, as we have seen, Heard was quoting Adolf Hitler, speaking on April 14, 1939, about Edward Benes, former president of Czechoslovakia.

Stanley Hoffman notes that the military approach has a long-standing precedent as an effective tool of the nation-state:

The "realist" orthodoxy insist that nothing has changed in international relations since Thucydides and Machiavelli: a state's military and economic power determines its fate; interdependence and international institutions are secondary and fragile phenomena; and states' objectives are imposed by the threats to their survival or security.[148]

However, there is increasing doubt on the effectiveness of the military trump card on economic activities as they become more intertwined, calling into question use of the military as global leaders, academics, and the media measure the results of the post–Iraq War reconstruction. It is difficult to predict the longevity of the military approach, but its use as an instrument for long-term stability is fueling new debates as expressed by Michael Kidron and Dan Smith:

The international military order, a hierarchy of power based on war, the threat of war and on permanent preparations for war, is one way of organising world affairs. It is not a productive, generous, humane or safe way. And it is not the only way. It is not often recognised for what it is: one of many options, created by the powerful for their own benefit and aggrandisement.[149]

Christopher Catherwood makes an important contribution to the dialogue on the effectivity of the military approach to foreign policy:

The Cold War was won, not by tanks and missiles, but by ideas. If we hold our ideas and values to be true, then we should want the Muslim world to be open to them if they are presented in a nonthreatening way. It often looks as if it is a choice between some unsavoury despotic regime and a crazed fundamentalist one. Policy has all too often been made on the basis of this false dichotomy.[150]

There is no doubt that military might–based economic arrogance has galvanized twenty-two developing nations into opposing World Trade Organization–proposed rules on investment, competition, trade facilitation, and transparency in government procurement; this became evident at the WTO meeting in Cancún in 2003.[151] Compounding the issue is a scenario in which the U.S. recoils from an arrogant economic stance and focuses on more-protectionist measures, laying the foundation for the prospect of an economic conflict with current and future trading partners.

To digress for only a moment, one must remember the Corn Laws of the eighteenth and nineteenth centuries in Britain, where the introduction of tariffs restricted the free flow of corn, wheat, barley, and oats, to and from foreign countries, in order to shield the domestic farmers from international competition. Beginning as a measure of assistance, the bureaucratization of the process resulted in elaborate procedures and specialized controls, which ultimately led to manipulation of peripheral economic activities that in turn instigated civil disturbances, sparking fear of an insurrection.[152] The British government at the time diffused the situation with wage subsidies, which led to expanded entitlement programs and spawned inter-program fraud, greater economic inequities, and civil unrest.

Ironically, protectionism—along with other mechanisms that increase the tension in international commerce, sometimes kindling trade wars—is not new. Transnational economic activity is analogous to a revolving door, not a floodgate or canal lock that can be regulated to restrict and expand the flow of goods, services, and capital as a means to punish or reward political friends and foes. One could argue that without a clear understanding and agreement about conducting the equitable exchange of goods and services—placing the economic activities of each nation on a level playing field—the economies of the world have the potential to form five diametrically opposed trading blocs: North America, the European Union, Asia, Islam, and South America. These regionalized trading blocs could be organized to simply foster trade that supports predefined special interests and domestic-centric agendas, creating, in turn, increased world tension. At the present, the only thing that prevents this from happening is a lack of organization between trade partners; a lack of coordination of trading activity; and a lack of synchronization of national goals and objectives between each nation-state operating within a certain region.

To avoid this potentially treacherous state of global economic activities, U.S. policies must reflect a higher degree of inclusiveness by taking into consideration foreign economic problems when formulating both foreign and domestic policies. More important, these considerations and subsequent policy decisions should resound with the same degree of transparency that the markets demand of corporate entities. Fadel Gheit (former Mobil chemical engineer), in an interview with the *Guardian*, got to the heart of the issues surrounding the turmoil in the Middle East when he summarized the situation thusly:

> *The Americans have nothing against the people of Iraq, but our way of life is dependent on 20m barrels a day, and half of it has to be imported. We are like a patient on oil dialysis. It's a matter of life and death. The smart people [in Washington] all know this, but it's not generally advertised on the kind of shows that most people watch: MTV and soap operas.*[153]

To global consumers, the actions that result from U.S. policies make an indelible impression from a perspective of the value proposition of the American brand, communicating that in order for the U.S. economy to stimulate growth, America must condition itself to be in a continual state of war, such as with the war on terrorism today.[154]

THIRTEEN

Good and Just Trade versus Evil and Unjust Commerce

A good scare is worth more to a man
than good advice.
—*Edgar Watson Howe*

SINCE THE END OF WORLD WAR II, THE WORLD ECONOMY HAS
seen rapid growth, including a continual rise in international trade,
due primarily to determined efforts to reduce trade barriers, along
with technological developments such as the Internet and electronic commerce. Although many developing countries or emerging nation-states have opened their local economies to improve
domestic economic development through increased international
trade, the trade barriers of the industrial nation-states, which focus
on agricultural products and labor-intensive manufacturing, limit
the benefits of trade. Theoretically, a developing nation should
have an advantage over industrial nations in agricultural production and by leveraging national assets; further trade liberalization
would facilitate an escape from acute poverty. However, the advent
of the Internet was not viewed by Americans as a mechanism to
engage global cultures in a dialogue; rather, its wide appeal was

seen primarily as a means to spread U.S. products and services to new markets, while promoting Western socio-economic values.

American ideals and values are indelibly impressed on the brand identity of their products and, more important, into the fabric of the U.S. value proposition. Interestingly, the neoconservative dogma is acting to diminish or devalue the U.S. value proposition when it erects barriers to commerce, such as in the financial services industry, which uses banking transactions as a means to filter out terrorist financing. One of the principal ideals of the U.S. value proposition is that institutions do not arbitrarily discriminate against individuals, corporations, or other legal entities. As the United States creates more terrorist-seeking financial legislation, such as the Customer Identification Program (Section 326 of the Patriot Act), it inadvertently places Americans on the slippery slope toward a resurgence of McCarthyism.

Global customers are presented with a surprising paradox in American social behavior: Individuals who are responsible for facilitating significant financial transactions—such as banking professionals, real estate agents, and automobile dealers—are now being pressed into service as pseudo members of law enforcement, urged to seek out terrorists and other illegal sources of funds.Looking at the implementation of this legislation from the outside, it is clear that the individuals responsible for moving these transactions through the various financial, legal, and commercial channels are now forced to prejudge the consumer's intentions. To people outside the United States, actively employing citizens to investigate and prejudge intent provides an ironic reminder of American sentiment toward Soviet society during the Cold War. In reality, all economic activity has the potential to be used to support terrorism; what is in question is the degree to which the consumer is intentionally trying to usurp the power of a nation-state.

In defense of the role that the neoconservatives have had in shaping U.S. policy, Gerard Baker rightly notes that the process began long before the current administration, reaching a state of legitimacy prior to the events of September 11, 2001.[155] Homi Bhabha agrees that the global perception of American economic imperialism existed long before the Bush administration and its policies, as he observed in 1994:

> *I am equally convinced that, in the language of international diplomacy, there is a sharp growth in a new Anglo-American nationalism which increasingly articulates its economic and military power in political acts that express a neo-imperialist disregard for the independence and autonomy of peoples and places in the Third World.*[156]

The question remains: Are American economic and commercial interests at risk in the long term? Will perceived American imperialism and protectionist foreign policies instigate boycotts of U.S. "icons," such as Levis, McDonald's, Pepsi, Ford, and Coca-Cola? Will this adversely affect international sales, or reduce foreign capital investments?

As various elements of the U.S. value proposition lose the luster displayed in previous generations of international commercial activity, global investors will undoubtedly reconsider the U.S. as a favored destination for investment. Daniel Altman notes:

> *Though the first military foray under the doctrine of pre-emption ended in victory, it still cost the American people*

a great deal. The consequences, along with the prospect of further military initiatives, are giving international investors pause as they decide where in the world to put their capital.[157]

One can argue that the implied military reprisals found in George W. Bush's rhetoric have sent the message to global consumers and nation-states that the U.S. does not give equal weight to external viewpoints when it comes to having a dialogue about cultural ideologies. This message is encapsulated in statements such as: "Over time it's going to be important for nations to know they will be held accountable for inactivity. You're either with us or against us in the fight against terror."[158] This hard-line approach leaves little room for interpretation, and communicates to investors that under certain conditions, their investments within the United States may not be secure if their country of origin or residence falls out of favor with the U.S. This perception, coupled with continued U.S. multinational business efforts to promote globalization, causes nations to become increasingly suspicious of U.S. intentions.

However, many investors continue to see the fundamental strength of the U.S. economy as sufficient to justify its place as the favored destination for capital. They see the flexibility of U.S. markets and the nation's prospects for growth as superior to those of Japan and Europe. Nevertheless, it is still far too early in the implementation cycle of recently passed legislation to accurately assess the long-term implications of foreign and domestic policy decisions on investor attitudes. As China and the European markets become technologically invigorated by continued investments in financial infrastructure, they become increasingly capable (at least in terms of potential) to leapfrog U.S. markets to facilitate global commercial activity, the only threat to their position being trade regulation and protectionism. [159]

If one considers that emerging economic interdependence is a process of consolidation, which in turn reduces the operating cost of global business, then a number of new issues must be addressed. Will a higher degree of economic dependency and financial integration affect all countries in an equitable manner, or will the process favor wealthier nation-states and further widen the gap between rich and poor nations? In a world of tightly integrated economies, events that occur in one nation-state can be rapidly felt in the economic activities in another, leading to a higher frequency of macroeconomic instability. One could argue that emerging nation-states may be placed at a disadvantage when they act to open markets and engage in commercial activities against the industrial nation-states, as noted by the International Monetary Fund:

> *". . . it has proven difficult to find robust evidence in support of the proposition that financial integration helps developing countries to improve growth and to reduce macroeconomic volatility. . . . Countries enjoy the benefits of financial integration once they cross a threshold in the soundness of their domestic monetary and fiscal policies and the quality of social and economic institutions."*[160]

Therefore, U.S. foreign policy makers must take determined steps to engage other nations in the world toward the establishment of "equitable trade," not simply toward liberalizing trade. Dominant nation-states such as the U.S. must place the needs of their indigenous people into the broader context of raising global living standards, and work to develop mechanisms that promote higher volumes of trade. The benefits of trade liberalization are compelling; evidence suggests that outward-oriented countries grow at much faster rates when they lower tariffs and open foreign direct investment.[161]

To place this issue into a business context, the world economy is similar to a corporation with many departments, all engaged in the production of a vast array of products. When a production group is not performing at its peak profitability, the management team, working in close association with the senior members of the production staff, comes together and formulates a strategy which results in one of two possible solutions: 1) closing down the production facility and abandoning the product due to irreparable problems; or, 2) composing a strategy to systematically address each problem, committing resources to correct them and establishing measures to monitor the variables within the production process in order to prevent the recurrence of an unprofitable state. Unfortunately, in the context of the global economy, a low-performing nation-state cannot simply be jettisoned or closed down.

Global Commerce Is Not a Bed of Roses

From the perspective of an emerging nation or developing regional economy, as global commerce becomes interdependent, a disastrous ripple effect could be a by-product of change. This is particularly true in industrial nations, where production creates a sense of potential economic stability, and any factor altering production rates is seen as a threat. One could argue that the industrial nations and other global authorities have an obligation to install an economic baffling system, similar to the mechanisms used to keep stock markets from imploding during sell-offs. Other factors to consider in the debate over good and equitable commerce is a legacy of national sentiment, which, although not a prerequisite for commercial activity, remains an integral part of how a nation-state interacts with the United States and other larger economic powers.

The attitude of a nation—or, more specifically, people within an ideology that may span national boundaries, such as Islam—sets the tone for how that nation engages in global commerce; respects the social constructs of other sovereign states; and acknowledges social and cultural differences as equal in importance to their own. For example, Catherwood brings to the forefront one element which drives the Islamic disconnection with Western societies:

At the heart of Islamic rage today is a profound sense of humiliation in the face of the West. President Bush and countless other Americans have asked, "Why do they hate us?" The answer is this sense of shame and loss, and the perceived global dominance of the West over the Islamic world.[162]

Islamic terrorist groups seek to redress this imbalance, which is now also a rising issue most recently voiced within the emerging nations during the Cancún meeting of the World Trade Organization in 2003. It is interesting to note that the ripples of economic discontent are not solely located outside the United States; within the U.S., super-retail stores such as Wal-Mart have decimated the demand for local mom-and-pop retail stores, thus creating a micro-example of the interactions between multinationals and local producers in emerging nations.[163]

The Economics of Terrorism

Economic activity, or the suppression of a social class by economic means, has always been a catalyst for social unrest. In 1773, the might of the British army and navy were overwhelming forces that clearly outmatched the colonies on the North American continent. The Boston Tea Party, as we have seen, could have been construed as an act of economic terrorism against the British. If we ignore the motivations of terrorism for a moment and focus on the economics of a terrorist act, we can see why the process is both effective and appealing to any group with a special interest. Terrorist acts have a high return on investment, low risk, little or no capital equipment, and are accomplished with a seemingly small investment when compared to the defense spending of any nation-state.

Let us consider the facts: Before 9/11, few universities, colleges, and/or high schools offered Islamic studies or provided courses which address the conflicts in the Middle East in any depth. Since 9/11, the world has a new appreciation for the issues in the region, especially the cultural clash between Islamic extremists and Western philosophies. The world also has a greater sense of insecurity, coupled with a renewed sense of fear. The total investment in the 9/11 tragedy may never be known in detail, but it can be estimated in the following oversimplification:

- recruit, feed, and house several dozen terrorists;

- pay for enrollment fees in several terrorist training institutions;

- purchase a few dozen domestic plane tickets; and

- execute the plan.

The total cost was less than 1 million U.S. dollars. If one considers that the goal of the attack was not simply to punish America, but also to increase global awareness of their cause (e.g., marketing and publicity), one can see how effective this act of terror was. A terrorist group cannot afford to purchase commercial media coverage to communicate their grievances, goals, and objectives. However, they do realize that the level of media attention that follows their actions is powerful; reports of their attack are quickly broadcast by an eager press corps, thereby lowering their marketing budget to zero. Compared to the U.S. defense budget and all the associated federal agency budgets that are connected—directly or indirectly—to maintaining domestic peace and tranquillity, the ROI is unmistakably compelling.

That said, the act of terrorism is an appalling use of resources and should be condemned at every opportunity; however, its economic effectiveness as a mechanism for global change cannot be ignored. Terrorism will continue to be the preferred method to bring about change until an equally effective alternative approach can be established. Terrorists and other extreme special interest groups, like consumers and business organizations, always strive to adopt a method that delivers maximum effect with minimum expense. The terror-based approach to global change stands in stark contrast to current national strategies for safety, defense, trade, and financial regulations, which, to the detriment of taxpayers, are based on massive spending for little or no economic gain. The effectivity of terrorism to promote global awareness of Islam has led many universities to create new Islamic studies programs, while the worldwide media has continued to raise awareness of the multicultural problems in the Middle East.

FOURTEEN

The Price of Freedom, Liberty, and Commerce

They that can give up essential liberty to obtain a little temporary safety deserve neither liberty nor safety.
—*Right-wing extremist Benjamin Franklin*

IN THE FINAL ANALYSIS, WE MUST LOOK AT HOW FOREIGN policy impacts its citizens; how it affects domestic commerce; and how it prepares the nation to embrace the next generation of global commercial activity. We must ask the question: Is the price for national security so high that it can only be achieved by the reduction of liberty within a nation-state? Historically, when national fears are aroused, civil liberties are often reduced, and any dissension is treated as unpatriotic.[(164)] Patriotism becomes a cloak which protects fearmongers from what is truly behind their actions: bigotry, hatred, and xenophobia. Freedom and liberty are not birthrights; they are privileges granted by an underlying social contract represented by the Constitution, the preservation of which requires constant vigilance. What is freedom? Modern dictionaries define freedom as: "The condition of being free of restraints; liberty of the person from slavery, detention, or oppression; exemption from the arbitrary exercise of authority in the performance of a specific action; civil liberty: *freedom of assembly, freedom of speech, freedom from unreasonable search and seizure."*

One could argue that acts of terrorism are devised to promote a political agenda in the Middle East, and that they are the ultimate expression of freedom, as they are performed by individuals acting beyond the restraints of socially acceptable behavior. However, these actions, regardless of their purpose, are not to be admired, condoned, or promoted, because they in turn violate the unwritten social contract between people living in a free society, and they compromise the liberty of others. This then raises the question: How can freedom be maintained internally within a nation, and with other sovereign states, without compromising the liberty, rights, and freedom of others?

Terrorism succeeds and enacts a toll on freedom, liberty, and economic stability only if the foreign policies of the economically dominant nation-states ignore the root causes of conflict and global discontent, fail to address the issues that act as a catalyst for terrorism, and submit to the fear designed by its creators. Noam Chomsky provides us with a sharper view:

> *We should also be able to appreciate recent comments on the matter by Ami Ayalon, the 1996–2000 head of Shin Bet, Israel's general security service, who observed that "those who want victory" against terrorism without addressing underlying grievances "want an unending war."* (165)

Chomsky rightly points out that acts of terrorism such as 9/11 are not simply intended toward individual Americans, but rather, are attacks against U.S. foreign policy that ignores the core problems. This includes developing an understanding between nation-states based on jettisoning special self-interest to establish a more comprehensive attitude toward trade and other aspects of economic activity that will in turn be a catalyst for a more equitable exchange of goods and services. However, economic equality is not always in the best interest of the U.S. Businesses have a lot to lose on a level playing field, where 50 percent of the world can offer lower wage rates. Thomas Paine noted in *Common Sense*: "The more men have to lose, the less willing are they to venture. The rich are in general slaves to fear, and submit to courtly power with the trembling duplicity of a spaniel." U.S. businesses have two great fears: fear of shareholders demanding better performance, and fear of international competition that can offer the same product at a fraction of American production costs. Therefore, international economic activity coupled with the influence U.S. business has on local cultures are at the heart of global dissidence.

Organizations such as the IRA, ETA ("Euskadi Ta Askatasuna," Basque for Basque Homeland and Freedom), and Al-Qaeda acquire their motivations from a wide range of issues that are exceedingly dissimilar, which points out a fallacy in the Bush administration's foreign policy: namely, that all terrorism is basically the same. The broad definition of terrorism found in sections 411 and 802 of the Patriot Act[166] has the potential, if misused, to allow the government to revoke some of the freedoms granted by the Constitution. One could argue that as a reaction to terrorism, the U.S. government (with other governments following suit) has created laws that put a huge premium on attaining a sense of national security; in fact, such a value is placed on security that conditions are created whereby special interest groups may no longer find it desirable to participate within the established boundaries of the political process. This, in turn, could lead to a self-fulfilling terrorist prophecy. The silent, steadfast, and subliminal erosion of freedom, liberty, and security comes from within a nation's legislative process (passing restrictive laws), and the executive process (lack of comprehensive foreign policy), not from the actions of external terrorists, as observed by Edmund Burke in the nineteenth century: "The true danger is when liberty is nibbled away, for expedience, and by parts."[167] This sentiment was echoed by James Madison in a letter to Thomas Jefferson on May 13, 1798: "Perhaps it is a universal truth that the loss of liberty at home is to be charged to provisions against danger, real or pretended, from abroad."[168]

The preservation of freedom, which is claimed to be at the heart of foreign and domestic policy, is found not in the erection of deterrents, but in the understanding of its root causes of social discourse, such as terrorism, and by addressing the issues that cause it to threaten the freedom of indigenous peoples. Terrorism has the explicit goal of altering the behavior of a target population by employing methods designed to destabilize their psyche, creating a state of fear. In effect, its aims are to reduce the attributes of freedom, such as travel, security, and the right to self-expression, all highly valued by the local citizens.

Moreover, the administration's use of fear to justify collecting vast amounts of information on its citizens (what they buy, where they go, who they talk to, and what they read) has also provided the necessary pretext for withholding information from the public under the umbrella of national security concerns.[169] The implicit goal of terrorism is to promote the agenda of the terrorist, which can be described as economic, cultural, political, military, nationalistic, or spiritual; this is the root cause of the terrorist act. The detrimental effects of terrorism on freedom are, by definition, part of the terrorist agenda, which leaves us in a catch-22 situation: Terrorism threatens our sense of security, thus increasing our belief that we need more security; additional security infringes on our individual freedom, therefore eroding the U.S. principle of liberty. Doesn't it feel like the terrorists win, either way?

Liberals argue that the development of more-stringent visa requirements for student and tourist entry will not deter terrorists, but instead, will only reduce the freedoms of, and further inconvenience, law-abiding citizens. Terrorists, who are trained to evade detection, will continue to escalate their efforts as the barriers to prevent entry continue to increase. Analogous to the buildup of weapons during the Cold War, the new restrictions will simply act as a catalyst for terrorists to become invisible, while at the same time, silently eroding freedom by permanently instilling a sense of fear in the population. Immigration is the foundation of economic growth, as it fosters the cultural diversity that is the cornerstone for a heterogeneous society. Actions by lawmakers—such as reforming the student visa program and visa overstays, at the heart of legislation such as the Enhanced Border Security and Visa Entry Reform Act of 2002[170]—is simply good public policy, and should not have to be linked to changes instituted because of terrorism.[171] The need for these reforms identifies the lack of a proactive comprehensive national policy, because it changes only after catastrophic events generate enough momentum to initiate reforms.

It can be argued that U.S. counterterrorism actions are an overreaction stemming from the sudden reality that America's multibillion-dollar defense budget can be easily breached by individuals, and not by sovereign states—the reason the defense systems were designed in the first place. The resulting legislation helps to advance the goals of terrorism by reinforcing the condition of fear, making citizens more aware of the vulnerabilities of national defense. To place this issue into a proper context, we must consider that individuals who subscribe to the beliefs of the society in which they live believe in and obey that society's laws. An individual accepts the laws that govern their actions because of a common understanding of the behavior required to participate in a free society. Terrorists and other individuals whose objectives are to *interrupt* domestic tranquillity simply ignore these laws, because to them, they hold no value.

Legislation enacted in response to the atrocities committed by terrorists unwittingly emphasizes the issue that is at the heart of the terrorist's implied goal, which is to alter the behavior of society. This influence is demonstrated in the opening sentence of the USA Patriot Act enacted by the 107th Congress: "To deter and punish terrorist acts in the United States and around the world . . . ,"[172] which confirms the primary issue in the terrorist's mind—that the U.S. wants to continue spreading its control over other nation-states. Seemingly, this language was interpreted as America using its military resources to impose its own values and beliefs on others, irrespective of the sovereignty of any other nation-state, and electing to take on the role of the world's police force.

FIFTEEN

The Next Wave of Commerce

THE LONG-TERM COMMERCIAL INTERESTS OF THE UNITED States must be managed by domestic and foreign policies that fully engage America in transnational commerce that is perceived as equitable by all international actors. To manage this process effectively, an administration must strike a balance between conservative and liberal views on trade, and consider factors outside the U.S. borders in a single global economy. Businesses can only operate for a short time without a strategy that leverages the value proposition of the goods and services offered to customers. Like business, the U.S. value proposition must be managed as a process, which views commercial activities from all nation-states as equal competitors and equal partners. In the business world, the phenomenon of *co-opetition* is emerging as a model that lowers cost, reduces risk, increases corporate agility, and enables businesses to participate in a network of value creation. The economic policies of the United States must also rise to engage all nation-states in global co-opetition, following two parallel paths: an *external perspective* that engages foreign nations and policy critics in a dialogue that promotes equitable trade relations; and an *internal perspective* that reassesses national self-interests against the backdrop of global citizenry. Corporations are increasingly aware of the rising consumer demand to become more responsive to local needs, which has resulted in an increased need for businesses to be perceived as responsible global citizens.[173]

When passing legislation that is designed to promote a domestic special interest, policy makers must consider the resulting international trade difficulties it poses to the U.S. value proposition, and consider the additional cost to businesses, or, ultimately, to consumers. Overregulation and legislation that is designed to thwart terrorism by sifting through billions of daily transactions will, over time, add incremental costs that will eventually result in a reduction in the price/performance of U.S. exports. These are stopgap measures that will ultimately need to be reconsidered in favor of a more-comprehensive strategy to reduce the cost of global commerce within the U.S., and, more important, to developing nation-states.

According to Lael Brainard, America's long-term security is dependent on wealthier nations lowering barriers to trade to make global commerce more inclusive:

> *Trade policy presents hard tradeoffs between, on one hand, the losses faced by those whose jobs and companies are vulnerable to international competition and, on the other hand, the greater but more diffuse national interest in a more competitive and productive economy—and in promoting a more peaceful, prosperous and equitable world.*[174]

The association of liberalized trade and job loss creates a paradox for Americans whose demand for cheaper imported goods is in sharp contrast to the reactions from business and voters, who argue for protectionist policies that promote job retention.[175]

Seemingly, the protectionist tenor of the Bush administration's foreign and domestic policies may be a natural but dangerous reaction to the current economic downturn following the dot-com meltdown on Wall Street. Protectionism places a nation on a precarious economic path that in the past has more times than not preceded global conflicts, such as when Britain abandoned free trade in 1931 in favor of a self-contained national economy, while the majority of nations retreated into a similar defensive posture, coming close to a policy of autarchy, mitigated by bilateral agreements.[176]

In the nineteenth century, the United States was presented with the challenge of rebuilding and unifying its national economy. To become a nation, it was necessary to establish a single currency and to regulate commerce using equitable mechanisms for intra- and interstate trade. Economic unification in the emerging industrial nation-state was not easy, nor was it quick. As we move further into the twenty-first century, the opportunity to facilitate global economic unification in an environment of fair and equitable trade is the challenge that the U.S. can reject for its own self-interest or embrace as a willing and active participant. The U.S. value proposition can be greatly improved by crafting actions that respond to three fundamental aspects of global commerce, as noted by Brooks and Wohlforth:

1) lowering domestic trade barriers to reduce friction and resentments generated by unipolarity;

2) moving beyond reacting to the challenges of national security and terrorism to address the root causes that have led to their emergence; and

3) setting an example by clearly demonstrating that the U.S. is willing to jettison its own special interests in favor of the interests of all nations.[177]

In the words of the nineteenth-century merchant, Richard Cobden, "The progress of freedom depends more upon the maintenance of peace, the spread of commerce, and the diffusion of education, than upon the labors of cabinets and foreign offices." Perhaps the most upbeat view of the challenges that await the new frontier of global commerce was best expressed by commissioner Mozelle W. Thompson of the U.S. Federal Trade Commission:

> *In a global marketplace it is important for all of us to work together, while at the same time to recognize that countries have different legal and value systems and therefore approach problems differently. Our differences, however, should be valued, and we should learn from each other in order to benefit consumers around the world.*[178]

Part IV:
Breaking the Cycle of Fear—
Can America Rebound?

Capitalism is the belief that the wickedest of men will do the
wickedest of things for the betterment of humanity.
—*John Maynard Keynes*

AMERICA IS NOT ALONE IN THE PROCESS OF INTERNALIZING
public fear. In the aftermath of 9/11, government policy makers
worldwide started accelerating plans and implementations of more-
sophisticated ways of tracking the movements of people within
their borders using new technology, such as secure national identification cards, biometric passports, and other means of monitoring
people. According to security industry consultant David Tushie:
"The use of these secure forms of ID will provide governments
with real-time data in the event of an act of terrorism, and can act
as a real deterrent to would-be evildoers."[179] Maybe ID cards will
even be able to fix global warming—who knows?

Sarcasm aside, if we consider how American business is adopting the use of language such as "real deterrent to would-be evildoers," one can see that the use of this type of language is a direct
reflection of the Bush administration's foreign policy of preemp-
tion. As a society, America has yet to understand the full implications of the rising anxiety within the nation. For example, Robert

Mandel notes that the collateral impact of individual responses to personal safety has a ripple effect within the community:

> On an individual level, seeing a home nearby put up a PRO-
> TECTED BY BRINKS HOME SECURITY SYSTEM sign in the front yard
> can foster a fresh sense of vulnerability among neighbors
> without one; on a group level, seeing a gated community
> erected or a private security force employed nearby can
> similarly make other groups increasingly vigilant to real
> or imagined threats from outside; and on a national level,
> seeing a proximate state resort to reliance on foreign pri-
> vate security forces to maintain or restore order can cause
> regional onlookers to worry more about the contagion of
> violence from the given state into their own borders.[180]

As Mandel rightly points out, fear triggered by the visible signs of others' fear, whether real or imagined, spreads fear to others who may not yet be aware that they are afraid.

Politicians have used the debate on the "digital divide" (access to computers and the Internet) during campaigns to garner support for their programs on education. The focus of the debate is a growing concern that people without access will become a disadvantaged class within society that will be left behind. One could argue that the same is true with security and societal anxiety, as people living in gated communities (typically at the higher end of the economic spectrum) are perceived to be safer than the average citizen.

Conceivably, as the media colludes to remind us of our fear, we have become a nation of watchers, or as Benjamin Barber, author of *Jihad vs. McWorld*, said:

America has become too much a nation of spectators. We watched the horror of 9/11 on TV over and over again. We watch politics on television instead of getting involved in politics. We will watch the war in Iraq, as we watched the war in Afghanistan, not as citizens but as spectators. The two are at the opposite ends of the civic spectrum. Citizens are active, engaged, responsible partners in changing the world for the better. Spectators merely watch the world happen to them. And, as a result, invariably they are fearful and anxious. Citizens, by contrast, are always fearless, not because they are without fear, but because in their activities and actions they have found a way to overcome fear.[181]

Our individualism and national sense of self is perchance a contributing factor to our lack of inaction in addressing world problems on an individual basis. Perhaps to remove ourselves from fear, we must simply turn off the television and get involved.

SIXTEEN

How Not to Be a Victim of Fear

To be afraid is to have more faith in evil than in God.
—Emmet Fox

Fighting terrorism is not simply about buying more surveillance technology or spending more money on the military or homeland security; it is about addressing the underlying root causes of what brings about terrorism. The reason terrorism occurs in America is because America is perceived to be a country that disregards other people in its pursuit of individualism and special interests, and does not live up to a higher set of global responsibilities. Al Gore's book, *The Assault on Reason*, describes the current fallacy of the U.S. government's use of fear:

> *Nations succeed or fail and define their essential character by the way they challenge the unknown and cope with fear. And much depends on the quality of their leadership. If leaders exploit public fears to herd people in directions they might not otherwise choose, then fear itself can quickly become a self-perpetuating and freewheeling force that drains national will and weakens national character, diverting attention*

*from real threats deserving healthy and appropriate fear
and sowing confusion about the essential choices that every
nation must constantly make about its future.*[182]

Gore rightly observes that as the government and media continue to use fear as a means of scaring us into justifying the actions
of government, the technique erodes the national character. If we
consider that for the most part, people agree that fear (or the perception of fear) is a by-product of government actions, can we say
that the development of fear is a *consequence* of their actions—or is
it the *intention* of their actions? Simply, do governments, business,
and the media consciously sit down and use fear as a key element
of their planning? For example, companies selling war insurance,
terrorism insurance, and political violence insurance use statistical probability models during the policy underwriting process,
which take into account a number of factors such as political risk,
property values, physical security, and levels of civil strife within
a geographical location. They subsequently use the fear of loss as
a mechanism to set the premium people pay for the policy. The
higher the fear, the more policies they write. In reality, only 31
Americans died in terrorist attacks domestically and abroad during
2002, which places the risk of being killed by a terrorist at 1 in 9.3
million. According to Michael Sivak and Michael Flannagan of the
University of Michigan, ". . . an American's chance of being killed
in one non-stop airline flight is about 1 in 13 million (even taking
the September 11 crashes into account). To reach the same level of
risk when driving on America's safest roads—rural interstate high-
ways—one would have to travel a mere 11.2 miles."[183]

Therefore, anxiety about terrorism is far out of proportion to
the actual risk, yet citizens and businesses have bought and con-

tinue to buy terrorism insurance. On the business side, financial, real estate, and health-care firms have been the primary buyers in the major U.S. metropolitan areas: Boston, New York, Washington, and Dallas. Interestingly, or perhaps tragically, your chances of being killed by a motor vehicle in the U.S. are 1 in 7,000. Terrorism insurance sales rise in lockstep with the media coverage of terrorist activity, regardless of where it occurs in the world. There is a symbiotic relationship between terrorist insurance policy underwriters and the media. Although it may not be collusion on their part, they do realize the impact that they have on altering human behavior.

To begin to break the cycle of fear, one must first understand the constructs used by a sender (politicians, the media, and business) to communicate their messages and alter one's behavior. Communicating fear is not simply a single transaction between the sender and the intended recipient. To make people afraid requires a dialogue consisting of three parts: *preparatory condition* (attack is imminent), *sincerity condition* (we are taking these steps to make you safer), and *essential condition* (unless you let us do this, more bad things will happen).[184]

Breaking the cycle thus starts with recognizing the first condition and placing it into a greater context. In business, we have learned that motivating people using fear is an outdated management practice from the manufacturing era, as observed by Lisa Aldisert: "If you don't produce x amount by y date, then you are on probation."[185] In Aldisert's view, managers who use fear tactics only motivate employees who are already afraid of losing their jobs. Talented employees are confident in both their ability to perform and their capacity to find another job. Today's progressive business leaders understand that using fear limits the productivity and innovation of a corporation, because fear of job loss or other reprisals simply causes employees to discontinue taking risks and stop thinking for themselves. Fearful employees become overly conservative, content with following the rules and not disturbing the status quo. Business leaders have learned that motivation is a process in which they must strike a balance between objectives and reward systems.

Striking a Balance

Political leaders must maintain a balance between security, danger, and freedom. Balancing this three-part equation is not easy because every society has some level of danger, whether it be car accidents, crime, forest fires, hurricanes, tornadoes, civil unrest, nuclear accidents, or wars. It is impossible to reduce danger in society to zero; therefore, the role of government is to provide an environment where real aggregate immediate danger is less likely and other dangers are minimized. Didier Bigo discusses this three-part equation in the context of European security/danger/freedom:

> Security is more like an expanding envelope, and insecurity [danger] is the environment in contact with this sphere, so the two phenomena expand at the same moment. More security may create more insecurity. Security may have negative connotations to freedom, but also to danger. Security is not always a "good thing" to "maximize."[186]

Bigo rightly points out that organizations mandated to protect a nation's freedom (police, Homeland Security, Immigration, and other agencies) see freedom as the management of fear and unease. Freedom is thus reduced to a physical place to protect, a place that is under threat (for example, a specific building or an airport needs to be protected and made secure). This simplification of freedom is a key step toward the suspension of civil liberties, as the defense against fear must take a physical form. This is all the more true today against non-state terror organizations than it was during the Cold War.

One point Bigo makes is that when it comes to an external threat, freedom and security must not be confused. To increase security in the name of protecting individual freedoms is simply an oxymoron. Nations should be empowered to allow the government to reduce individual freedoms for a limited period (a limited state of alert), but this state of alert cannot be seen as an unending condition. To declare, as President Bush has, that the United States is in a continual state of combat during the war on terrorism is to subvert the *raison d'être* of the government, as it is the function of the government to bring the nation back to stability; and once stable, liberty has to be restored. What America has to understand is that once the threat is no longer imminent, increased security simply creates more anxiety, a state whereby all individuals are terrorized—not by the actual terrorists, but by the image of a threat. And those selling this image, the fear merchants, are the ones perpetrating terrorism. You don't need an actual attack when the population is already in a continual state of terror.

The Homeland Security Advisory System is perhaps the most visible mechanism of perpetuating fear. Since its inception in March 2002, the threat level has only been raised to *Severe* (red) once, from August 10, 2006, through August 14, 2006. Responding to an announcement that British law enforcement had disrupted a major terrorist plot to blow up aircraft, the Department of Homeland Security raised the threat level for commercial flights from the United Kingdom to the United States to *Severe*. The threat level has been raised to *High* (orange) five times during its history on a nationwide level:

- September 10–September 24, 2002, around the first anniversary of the September 11, 2001 attacks.

- February 7–February 27, 2003, near the end of the Muslim religious holiday Hajj. Intelligence reports suggested the potential of terrorist attacks against non-secure targets (buildings, schools, hospitals).

- March 17–April 16, 2003, around the beginning of U.S. and Coalition military action in Iraq.

- May 20–May 30, 2003, after the Riyadh compound bombings and the Casablanca bombings, as the U.S. Intelligence Community claimed that Al-Qaeda entered an operational period worldwide, with high potential of attacks to the U.S..

- December 21, 2003–January 9, 2004, citing Intelligence information suggesting large-scale attacks around the holiday season.

In addition, the alert has been raised to *High* on a selective or partial basis three times:

- August 1–November 10, 2004, for specific financial institutions in northern New Jersey, New York, and Washington,

D.C., citing Intelligence reports that pointed to the possibility of truck bomb attacks, naming a number of buildings as possible targets.

- July 7, 2005–August 12, 2005, for mass transit systems only. The DHS secretary announced the high probability of attack against the U.S. after the 7/7 London bombings.

- August 10–14, 2006, for all domestic and international airlines with flights to or from the United States, with the exception of flights from the United Kingdom to the United States.

The State of the Nation's Fear:
The First 2,000 Days of the Homeland Security Advisory System

Threat Level	Risk	Days of risk
Severe (red)	severe risk	1
High (orange)	high risk	5
Elevated (yellow)	significant risk	1,994
Guarded (blue)	general risk	0
Low (green)	low risk	0

Figure 6. Homeland Security Advisory System (First 2,000 Days).

Perhaps the more significant fact is that the Homeland Security Advisory System (according to our research) has never been lowered to *Guarded* (blue) or *Low* (green). This raises an important question: Can one interpret this as 2,000 days of fear; and will we ever feel safe again? The most compelling aspect of the system is the use of language as seen in figure 7, from the Department of Homeland Security Website, September 6, 2007:

The United States government's national threat level is Elevated, or Yellow [An elevated condition is declared when there is a significant risk of terrorist attacks]. However, there continues to be no credible, specific intelligence to suggest an imminent threat to the homeland at this time.[187]

Figure 7. Homeland Security Advisory System (September 6, 2007).

It is interesting to note that while the advisory says the threat level represents a significant risk of terrorist attacks, they later qualify the elevated threat level by saying there is no imminent threat to the homeland at this time. Which way is it? Are we at risk, or aren't we? The message the government is trying to portray is simple: The risk is elevated *every* day. We will never be a nation at rest—or at peace, or safe—again.

What to Do?

Americans are afraid; they are told that there is good reason to be afraid. Of course, following 9/11, the U.S. has invaded two countries; expanded its reach toward Europe for support, blatantly criticizing nations such as France, where support was not granted; sent troops around the world, from Somalia to the Philippines, to fight Islamic militant extremists; and is threatening to attack any nation harboring terrorists.[188] The question is—Shouldn't the rest of the world be afraid of the U.S.?

What can Americans do to get a grip on reality and understand that living in fear and relinquishing liberty and control to the government is not a solution? America is a nation built on the existence (peaceful, at most times) of different nationalities, diverse religions, and dissimilar ethnic groups. America is a melting pot. The reason why America is great is because Americans accept the differences and understand the need to be a diverse environment. Just like an ecosystem needs different species to survive, so does America. Alienating parts of the population and isolating itself from the other nations is not the solution. Instead, Americans should undertake the mission to embrace differences and to be more proactive toward building not only a greater, fairer society, but also, a fairer world.

Americans should abandon their fear and the irrational feeling that the world hates Americans. They should travel and see the world, to understand how other cultures live and prosper—even those where the political systems do not match America's idea of the best system of government. No one can prevent the individual actions of a handful of people who aim to cause terror, yet more people die in car accidents every year than they ever will by terrorist attacks. If people do not quit driving or go into a nervous fit every time they turn their keys in the ignition, then there is really no reason to become afraid when entering an airport. What made the American nation great can just as easily bring about its downfall; the pioneering American spirit of exploring new lands and expanding beyond the easy reaches of geography can become an arrogant attitude of "We are better than others." What America needs to do, as it always has, is to understand the differences of others, and respect them. This is really the only way to stop animosity and belligerence, resume diplomacy, and become unafraid.

Conceivably, the most important thing individual Americans can do is to hold their leaders accountable for their actions by engaging in critical debate. In order to do this, Americans must be able to identify when fear is used in the construction of public policies. For example, a foreign policy constructed around an agenda of fear has a unique set of characteristics: it is overreactive; "black or white" (you are either with us or against us); it describes an enemy in broad or vague terms; it asks people to put aside their liberties temporarily; and it contains rhetoric that sounds similar to "the ends justify the means." Effective foreign policy calls for dialogue between nations to build alliances, trust, and understanding, while fostering hope and collaboration between economic partners. More important, when public policies are based on fear, they become self-fulfilling prophecies, as they internalize the threat which is the objective of terrorism.

SEVENTEEN

An Inconvenient Truth and the Convenient Enemy

We will not be driven by fear into an age of unreason
if we dig deep in our history and doctrine and remember
that we are not descended from fearful men, not from men
who feared to write, to speak, to associate, and to defend
causes which were, for the moment unpopular.
—*Edward R. Murrow (reporting on Senator Joseph McCarthy in 1954)*

IF ONE CONSIDERS THE NEXT LOGICAL STEP IN SECURING THE "freedom of place," as described by the organizations that are empowered to protect our freedom, one can be sure that it is the erection of physical or virtual barriers within the United States. Although capable of making the nation allegedly safer, erecting checkpoints between states to monitor the movement of people (suspected terrorists, drug dealers, organized crime, sex offenders) is probably not economically viable in the long term. However, mandating that a radio frequency identification (RFID) chip be placed under everyone's skin and subsequently monitoring them by stations linked via a telecommunications infrastructure would accomplish the same end goal at a lower operating cost. Protecting the physical environment is the new benchmark of security—but what about freedom?

Another transgression could be that the environment itself becomes the focus of an imagined fear. The environment is the new enemy; as people come to fear global calamity, they more easily justify government spending, which thus stimulates the economy just as the space program did during the Cold War.

During the Cold War, millions of people in the West feared communism. In 1989, the Iron Curtain fell from within. Tanks, nuclear missiles, military technology—none of these (let alone World War III) were necessary to overthrow communism in East/Central Europe. In fact, one could argue that it was citizen power that finally did the trick. In other words, what we do can and does make a difference. The citizens of Prague in 1989 took risks in their protests. In the U.S., we are living in a democracy, and in theory, our protests are protected by the right to free speech. Politicians, the media, and big business all depend on their voters, viewers, and consumers to get reelected or to stay in business. In Britain, one tabloid newspaper back in the 1990s accused the City of Liverpool (home of the Beatles) of loutish, antisocial behavior as a city. Thousands of readers boycotted the newspaper, and sales plummeted. The newspaper ultimately had to apologize, which demonstrates the power of citizens and consumerism at work.

You do not have to go to Washington to change the world. Those who use fear, in fact, fear exposure themselves: loss of votes, loss of audience share, loss of sales. They exploit our fear, but they also have a fear of personal failure. Mass consumerism does not have to be organized into big rallies or protests to be effective. The power to change the conditions that breed fear lies in the individual; all you have to do is make an effort—turn off the television, get off the Internet, get a passport, and see the world. See for yourself, and take action. When you are watching the news and the anchor says phrases like, "What the president is trying to say is . . . ," or "What that really means is . . . ," an alarm bell should go off in your head, telling you to turn off the volume and think for yourself.

Do people stop driving because of car accidents? No; we still drive. So why do people stop flying when terrorists use planes? As we saw earlier, people after 9/11 canceled flights, took trains, drove their cars, or stayed home. They gave the terrorists a major victory by giving in to their fears and changing their travel patterns. Yet, in fact, we are still far more likely to die in a car than in a plane. How many planes have been destroyed by terrorists since 9/11? None. How many people have died in car accidents? Thousands. According to the insurance industry, you are far more likely to be killed in a car accident than if you were flying on a plane and there was a 9/11-type incident every month of every year. If we need a rational fear, being in a car should be a prime candidate.

Beware of Global Warming

Perhaps one of the biggest emerging fearmonger groups is the environmentalist movement. A rising number of scientists are now rebutting the science behind Gore's *An Inconvenient Truth*. To any scientist, the scientific method of having others review, duplicate, and comment on one's discoveries is a welcome exercise in the verification process. Regardless of the science behind *An Inconvenient Truth*, one thing is clear: The film is designed to scare people into action. Fear of rising sea levels, fear of vanishing polar bears, fear of increased hurricane activity, fear of more tornadoes—the list of catastrophes is almost endless. Perhaps a name more aptly suited for Gore's infomercial should be *A Convenient Fear* because of the numerous ways it is designed to scare people. If Alfred Hitchcock was alive today, he would be envious of the film. Whether the science behind the movie is right or wrong is immaterial, because the film very cleverly contains one word which is used as the greatest escape clause in the history of science: the word *if*. If the facts of the movie are true, be afraid; if the facts of the movie are false, be more afraid of how easily people are misled and how quickly people will spend money to placate their fears.

If you really want to be afraid, you should take a few minutes to read the Department of Defense–commissioned report on global climate change, *An Abrupt Climate Change Scenario and Its Implications for United States National Security*, developed under the concept of "Imagining the Unthinkable":

> *Violence and disruption stemming from the stresses created by abrupt changes in the climate pose a different type of threat to national security than we are accustomed to today. Military confrontation may be triggered by a desperate need for natural resources such as energy, food, and water rather than by conflicts over ideology, religion, or national honor.*[189]

Our intent with this book was to show how fear has been used and continues to be used as an intrinsic part of America's implementation of democratic free-market capitalism by the government, big business, and the media. Is there a global conspiracy? As historians and business thinkers, we are not in a position to judge, until perhaps the events have unfolded and we can reflect on them in hindsight. What is clear is that these three economic actors use fear to promote their agendas; whether or not there is collusion on their parts is immaterial in the context of our discussion. Now, you, the reader, must decide the level of credibility in our argument to determine, for yourselves, what actions should be taken to circumvent the use of fear in this manner. Since the use of fear derives its power from a departure of rational reasoning, one must look at action in a highly personalized context. Do you accept the status quo, or do you move toward radicalism or conservatism?

In our opinion, the true victim in the use of fear is personal liberty. One must remember that when you alter your behavior because of terrorism, the terrorists have won; when you alter your behavior to comply with the people fighting terrorism, the terrorists have also won.

Foreign policy must be structured in a greater context of advancing the world toward holistic economic success, not simply as a vehicle for promoting U.S. interests. The macroeconomic value that the U.S. has brought to the world markets in the past has been defined by the American consumers, delivered by U.S. businesses, and promoted by the U.S. government. As nation-states strive for economic synergy based on heterogeneous foreign and monetary policies, one could argue that in the near future, the value proposition of the U.S. will be defined by world markets in the same way that corporations' value propositions are defined by the customers they serve. Similarly, just as value in business is defined by customers, criticisms of U.S. policies must be viewed in the context of what these groups are trying to accomplish, and what purposes the policies fulfill. Government policies are often application-specific, to promote a predefined end, or based on reactions to world events. Reactionary policies are often repealed years later when their impact is fully assessed and better understood. That said, today's economic policies reflect a determined isolationism, exclusively designed to promote American interests. The net effect is a steady decline in the perception of the U.S. value proposition, demonstrated in the growing negativity toward the U.S. and American businesses throughout the world.[190]

In his candidacy announcement speech in Cedar Rapids, Iowa, on June 12, 1999, George W. Bush said: "I'll work to end tariffs and break down barriers everywhere, entirely, so the whole world trades in freedom. The fearful build walls. The confident demolish them. I am confident in American workers and farmers and producers. And I am confident that America's best is the best in the world." Yet America's policies and subsequent actions have been to fortify our borders as a fog of fear enables government to take on new powers in order to address temporary emergencies.

Exclusivity and isolationism in a rapidly globalizing world are the opposite of what the world's leading superpower should be professing. Foreign policy needs to be based on economic inclusion, collaboration, and the achievement of joint economic goals. The United States and the G7 nations should strive to develop economic synergies as a substitute for future conflicts. For example, the level of political interactions between the U.S. and Pakistan in the war on terror should be used in conjunction with the growing economic activity between the U.S. and India, to move these two populous countries away from confrontation and toward pragmatic collaboration.[191]

The Continued Use of Fear

The increasingly popular approach used by political leaders, environmentalists, and other special interest groups is to use fear in the same way that American public health promotion campaigns are typically designed to elicit fear. The use of fear to engage the American public has been effective in the short term; however, the long-term use of fear, similar to what has been learned in the health-care field, is often ineffective in achieving the desired behavioral change. In a 1998 article in the *American Journal of Public Health*, R. F. Soames Job wrote:

> *Campaigns which attempt to use fear as part of a punishment procedure are unlikely to succeed. Consistent with established principles of learning, fear is most likely to be effective if the campaign allows for the desired behavior to be reinforced by a reduction in the level of fear. This entails five requirements: 1) fear onset should occur before the desired behavior is offered; 2) the event upon which the fear is based should appear to be likely; 3) a specific desired behavior should be offered as part of the campaign; 4) the level of fear elicited should only be such that the desired behavior offered is sufficient to substantially reduce the fear; 5) fear offset should occur as a reinforcer for the desired behavior, confirming its effectiveness. Under some circumstances it may be difficult to ensure that these requirements are met. In general, a positive reinforcement approach may prove to be more effective than the use of fear.*[192]

In the Middle East, closer to the turmoil in the region, people are generally more aware of imminent danger. However, anyone traveling between the U.S. and countries like the United Arab Emirates can clearly see a surprising difference in the attitudes of the people. In places like Dubai, crime is minuscule by Western standards; there is a social sense of a bright future as the first metropolis being built from scratch in the twenty-first century rises from the desert. Economic activity is booming, young people are engaged, and the spirit of entrepreneurism is almost electric. Where is the fear? The greatest fear is that the economic boom might slow down, or that the shortage of materials (such as window glass and concrete) will interrupt the twenty-four-hour-a-day, seven-days-a-week construction industry. This same national spirit held by local Emirates and the sizable expatriate populations is reminiscent of America in earlier decades, where large civil engineering projects provided hope, and a vision of a better future. In the Middle East, where democratic capitalism is not the prevailing economic/political structure, we are witnessing a complete renaissance in cities such as Abu Dhabi, Doha, Dubai, Manama, Kuwait City, and Riyadh, all growing at astounding rates with less fear of the future than is found in Western democracies.

EIGHTEEN

Rekindling the American Spirit

Freedom is actually a bigger game than power. Power is what you can control. Freedom is about what you can unleash.
—*Harriet Rubin*

One could argue that the progress of global socioeconomic conditions preordains America's emerging role as the world-policing body and regulator of global commerce. Simply, the American administration, regardless of political party, is destined to follow a course similar to the economic decline of Great Britain during the twentieth century, as China emerges as the next economic powerhouse. The shift in U.S. policy to a more preemptive approach to terrorism at first appeared to be a straightforward response to the events of September 11. However, it is becoming increasingly clear that this response is a characteristic, next logical step in a progression of policy decisions, which were established long before the Bush administration. The seeds for this posture were sown earlier by President Kennedy's actions in the Cuban Missile Crisis, and later refined during the Reagan administration, with the signing of the National Security Decision Directive 138 (NSDD138), which, as Neil Livingstone points out, according to

Noel Koch: ". . . represents a quantum leap in counterterrorism, from the reactive mode to recognition that proactive steps are needed."[193]

Although steps were taken to thwart terrorism, the effectivity of these measures is debatable, as noted by Marc Celmer: "Despite all of its harsh rhetoric, the Reagan administration's approach has had no positive impact on the deterrence, prevention, and suppression of international terrorism, nor has it created a greater degree of safety for Americans traveling and living abroad."[194] One could argue that fighting the terrorism of non-state actors is predicated on personal beliefs and values not easily identifiable from citizen to citizen, making the target (or reprisals) difficult to identify. The ubiquity of terrorist thinking and its counterpart, the equally ubiquitous generation of fear, limits a nation's ability to mount countermeasures, because fear can be exacted anytime, anywhere, and by any means. For example, simply mailing several hundred letters to bureaucrats in Washington, sprinkled with Johnson's Baby Powder, will effectively shut down the government for a period of time; repeated applications will result in a lowering of the threat to routine, at which time the system then becomes vulnerable again.

Looking into the future, unless a process is established that demonstrates progress toward resolving political issues raised by all parties in the Middle East (and other areas of the world), terrorism will continue to be a feasible means of forcing political change, simply because it is economically viable.

Terrorism is the result of individuals striking back against a perceived enemy because traditional channels for international change have proved to be ineffective. Although it would be naive to think terrorism is simply a form of violent complaint, it does demonstrate the intensity of an individual's commitment to a given cause. Unfortunately, the current escalation of violent actions and the rising effectivity of terrorism as a means to initiate global change raises more questions than it provides answers, such as: How can the U.S. work toward achieving global stability? What can ordinary people do to promote change? What key aspects of foreign and domestic policy need to be readdressed? Can a hegemonic superpower be benevolent?

Does the U.S. have a clear role in nation building, or, more important, does the UN? The United Nations periodically establishes an International Security Assistance Force (ISAF) as a precursor to nation building by extending peacekeeping missions, such as in Afghanistan, sanctioned by the UN Security Council (UNSCR 1386) on December 20, 2001. The principal task of the ISAF in concert with the interim Afghan government is threefold: 1) to aid the interim government in developing national security structures; 2) to assist the country's reconstruction; and 3) to assist in developing and training future Afghan security forces.[195]

Perhaps the person who best understood a degenerative national condition before it came to pass was Margaret Chase Smith, who at the advent of McCarthyism, sensed the long-term implications of paranoid thinking when she addressed the U.S. Senate on June 1, 1950:

> *I would like to speak briefly and simply about a serious national condition. It is a national feeling of fear and frustration that could result in national suicide and the end of everything that we Americans hold dear. It is a condition that comes from the lack of effective leadership in either the Legislative Branch or the Executive Branch of our Government.[196]*

Senator Smith was responding to congressional actions that were approaching an almost witch hunt–like fervor, which in turn sparked national behavior that encouraged people to report on potential communists who appeared to be lurking at every door. In Smith's view, the ensuing national obsession with communism and anticommunist activities had begun long before McCarthy, and was playing into the designs of communism to confuse, divide, and conquer. Today, Americans must ask themselves: Are we now in the early stages of forming a society that is as obsessed with terrorism as our grandparents were fixated on communism? In their 1956 book, *Empire of Fear*, authors Vladimir and Evdokia Petrov describe life in the former Soviet Union as being under a regime of universal fear, where one in ten citizens was a government informant, spying and reporting on their neighbors.[197] This image of Russia during that time evokes an emotional response from many Americans (especially those of us who can remember "duck and cover" drills in school), who could not imagine living under a system where there was a lack of a fundamental trust between neighbors. Nonetheless, five decades later, the U.S. government now asks us to participate in similar acts when it enlists real estate agents to report their suspicions about potential homeowners who have large cash down payments.

Should Americans Fear Islam?

According to Vincent Cornell, who examined the motives of suicide bombers: "Hopelessness and despair have long been regarded as major sins in Islam, because they imply a lack of faith."[198] Nevertheless, hopelessness and despair are the conditions created in many emerging nations as a direct result of American intervention.

This is not only true in Islamic nations. Africa is a simmering cauldron of despair, where the progress of development is minuscule when contrasted against the demand from citizens and their rising expectations. For example in Accra, Ghana, the demand for affordable housing amounts to approximately 500,000 homes, while the combined output of the building industry and government construction of affordable homes is roughly 5,000 units. This translates into a hundred-year waiting list for a person to go from slum dwelling to a decent home.

Here again, America's foreign policy needs to address the fundamental economic conditions that subjugate the economic activities of other nations. According to Bhikhu Parekh:

When people are embittered and brutalized and prepare to throw away their lives, nothing we do to them will terrorize and deter them. Whatever we do to them only confirms their poor opinion of us and hardens their resolve. There is a limit to what we can do to intimidate and terrorize potential terrorists, and once these are exhausted, we are left without resources.[199]

In Parekh's view, the United States must create a "psychology of fear" in order to maintain a deep respect for American military power; over time, this punitive approach mirrors that used by its terrorist enemies.

Non-Americans reading this book must remember three of the basic tenets of American free-market capitalism: choice, profit, and proliferation. One could argue that the next generation of terrorism will move from acts of violence to economic actions. As information technology becomes more ubiquitous throughout the world, coordination of transnational acts of economic defiance become easier. For example, with much of the U.S. debt under the ownership of foreign governments, a coordinated sell-off could trigger huge economic consequences, sending a clear message of disapproval of U.S. policy moves. Let's watch Americans react when you hit them in the wallet. This raises the question: What if, in response to U.S. actions against Iraq's sovereignty, the world decided to stop buying American products? Or made a conscious decision to turn off the supply of oil or other commodity for a specific period, in order to retaliate economically instead of militarily?

Foreign Policy, the Economy, Big Business, the Media, and You

What is missing from foreign policy today is *dialogue*. Dialogue in this context is a bidirectional communication designed to achieve economic, monetary, and fiscal policy synchronization that acts to move all nations equally toward a specific set of goals and objectives. Policy makers will argue that such synchronization already exists, and in theory, that is true; however, in practice, policy synchronization is far from its theoretical constructs. Americans need to hold politicians accountable to a higher standard, rather than allowing them to simply preserve American interests, maintain protectionism, or facilitate the agenda of special interest groups. Based on our interactions with other nations, taxpayers should be asking: Is the American superpower helping to make the world a better place to live? The key to breaking this cycle of foreign policy based on "fear of punishment" is to develop one that reflects "hope of reward." This is problematic because the "hope of reward" model requires a vision of the future that would be acceptable to numerous nation-states. To gain global consensus requires a great deal of effort, understanding, and diplomacy.

The founding fathers of the United States realized that the union could be undermined if a fear seized the public imagination, thus ruling out a direct democracy in favor of a representative democracy.[200] In *The 9/11 Commission Report*, deputy secretary of state Richard Armitage communicated his worries that the U.S. was "exporting our fears and our angers, not our vision of opportunity and hope."[201] One must remember that terrorism is, after all, psychological warfare that is only effective when the society internalizes events like 9/11 and allows them to develop into an irrational fear.

Louise Richardson makes a good observation on the relativity of the 9/11 tragedy, pointing out that 900,000 Americans died in 2001: 131,117 of acute causes; 42,000 (of which 17,500 were alcohol-related) in automobile accidents; 30,000 suicides; 16,000 homicides; and 15,000 from falls.[202] Richardson rightly points out that although equally as tragic, the approximately 3,000 people who died in 9/11-related events was a small percentage in comparison to other U.S.-based tragedies; for example, in 2001, six times as many people died as a result of drunk driving. Amplified by the media and the politicians, 9/11 has become proportionally overemphasized, purely to justify a political agenda centered on vengeance and inspired by fear. Terrorism, after all, is the ultimate misuse of fear for political ends. Indeed, its specific goal is to distort the political reality of a nation by creating fear in the general population, which is hugely disproportionate to the actual danger that the terrorists are capable of posing.

Perhaps the most important aspect (and least understood by the average American) is the impact our post-9/11 actions is having on the attitudes of people throughout the world. The Pew 2006 Global Attitude Survey asked 1,700 people in 15 countries their opinion on the following question: "[Did] the war in Iraq to remove Saddam [make] the world . . . a safer place, [or a] more dangerous [one]?" An overwhelming 73 percent of the respondents indicated that they believed the world is more dangerous today, with only 27 percent believing the world is safer. A growing popular opinion in Europe, Africa, the Middle East, and more recently, Asia, is that the United States has become the most serious threat to world peace and economic stability. Moreover, what this decline in attitude will equate to in the future is an erosion of the U.S. value proposition in the form of lower demand for U.S. goods and services, and perhaps, less availability of raw materials, as foreign businesses seek new trading partnerships.

Security is a prudent measure, allowing all societies to maintain order from terrorist sources, both foreign and domestic. However, an overemphasis on security and the establishment of a continuous state of vigilant alert simply creates a sense of heightened anxiety that is counterproductive, and has long-term consequences. Our nation has gone through other periods in our history when the misuse of fear resulted in abuses of civil liberties. The Alien and Sedition Acts of 1798 through 1800, the Palmer Raids, and the Red Scare after World War I. During World War II, the internment of Japanese Americans was another shameful episode, followed by the McCarthy abuses of the Cold War period. After each of these eras of excess, we as a nation felt ashamed, and tried to make up for the abuses, with monetary payments in some cases, with apologies, with new laws and new protections. And although we have not yet entered the period of regret and atonement this time around, it is already obvious that we are now in one of those periods of regrettable excess.

Richard Nixon said, "People react to fear, not love. They don't teach that in Sunday school," he said, "but it's true." Within the rubric in which foreign policy is designed to give people the illusion of safety (to subdue their fears), while simultaneously supporting key economic interests of the United States, is the reimagining of America. The establishment of the Department of Homeland Security brings forth an image of domestic space (where Americans are safe at home), and at the same time, portrays an image that foreign lands are not safe—indeed, that they are hostile and unfriendly.[203] What Americans fail to see is the parallelism of what is happening today within the nation and historical precedents in other nations, such as the similarity between concepts of the American homeland and the German fatherland.

The unasked question is whether this is the resurgence of a process that starts with the rooting out of suspected terrorists (or individuals that may have a tendency toward terrorism) and ends with the development of an anti-immigration national attitude. The fundamental concept that Americans must come to terms with is that the use of the word *homeland* constitutes a dichotomy in images: of *inside* (safe) and *outside* (fear) the boundaries of the United States. Amy Kaplan observes that this codification relies on America being in a continual state of war, whereby homeland security is dependent on a sense of insecurity, thus transforming the homeland itself into the battlefield of terrorism.[204] In Kofi Annan's Nobel Prize acceptance speech, he notes: "New threats make no distinction between races, nations, or regions. A new insecurity has entered every mind, regardless of wealth or status."[205]

The Cold War doctrine was based on deterrence by fear, each side equally horrified at the thought of mutually assured mass destruction. Prevention of nuclear war rested on diplomatic options under a framework of increasingly deadly scenarios. Clearly this military one-upmanship philosophy has little effect on a war on terror with non-state actors. Thus, foreign policy must holistically address the root causes of terrorism in order to be effective, not simply provide an impenetrable barrier of physical and economic isolationism. One does not have to subscribe to conspiracy theories to understand the role fear plays in shaping American attitudes toward foreign policy. What is needed, according to Zachary Selden, director of the Defense and Security Committee of the NATO Parliamentary Assembly, is "an appreciation of the core ideals that have guided it [America] over the years and how those ideals differ from what is found in European political thought."[206]

What is needed in today's foreign policy is perhaps a reacquaintance with the ideals that forged the original American spirit. As a policy of isolationism looms and the U.S. continues to erect numerous physical and electronic barriers to scrutinize, monitor, and prevent an infiltration in America by foreign people that may pose a threat (real or imagined), one cannot forget that America is a nation built on immigration. When visitors to the U.S. stand in line at airport security and witness the process of security and immigration, it must be a terrific shock as a first impression of the land of the free. Many of us who grew up in America can remember our first trip to see the Statue of Liberty in New York. On the pedestal is perhaps one of the most moving poems in history, which, in the post-9/11 world of fear, seems like a vanishing memory, or perhaps, a fading dream:

> *Give me your tired, your poor,*
> *Your huddled masses yearning to breathe free,*
> *The wretched refuse of your teeming shore.*

Send these, the homeless, tempest-tost to me,
I lift my lamp beside the golden door![207]

A New Foreign Policy

Much can be said about the biological effects of fear. Indeed, the human brain and body react to fear in a particular manner, with a form of reactionary panic that eventually disperses into a memory of the event which triggered the fear attack.[208]

We believe it is safe to say that the current U.S. foreign policy was created in the panic stage; as we have shown above, this panic stage has not yet dissipated into memory. America sees itself as being under a constant and permanent threat. As a result, foreign policy makers are unable to move past the initial stages of fear to create a strategy which looks beyond the potential threats, to seek to improve the international challenges which cause the aforementioned threats.

Foreign policies should include a number of elements in their formulation that are selfish (concerned with protecting the nation), but also some that are selfless (aiming to accept each other's differences and move on). The current U.S. foreign policy is based on the principle of Contending and Avoiding (America choosing to fight, or, when impractical, to isolate nations and create sanctions between friendly nations and the enemy). The U.S. foreign policy should not focus on saving America from its enemies; rather, it should focus on Accommodating, Collaborating, and Compromising. Americans should not fight the enemy for fear that the enemy will attack them; instead, they should try and understand *why* the enemy is attacking in the first place. What America needs to do to become a friendly nation is to stop focusing exclusively on itself and start trying to understand the rest of the world.

The American democratic system is one of its best qualities. The Constitution protects anyone who expresses an opinion, so why not take advantage of this to increase awareness about world hunger, poverty, and the lack of economic, social, and political development outside American borders? In short, you cannot expect the world not to turn its back on you if you turn your back on the world. This is the root problem in America at the moment, and why it is under attack. Heightened security does not address the causes of the problem; it is merely a reactive Band-Aid solution for a crisis that is not being fixed. Can America learn to be proactive instead of preemptive?

The new doctrine of U.S. foreign policy should be inclusive of the economic needs of other nations; this is not to say that future foreign policy should be based on a continuous stream of foreign aid. Quite the opposite; emerging nations are not looking for handouts from G7 nations (now G8 nations!); what they require is a level playing field for their own goods and services, in addition to access to foreign markets. A viable export from the U.S. to world governments is access to best practices in business, government, and societal infrastructure. Here again, foreign governments are not interested in Americanizing their economies; they are interested in making their economies more efficient and less corrupt. They simply want to make their nations better places for their people to strive for their own version of life, liberty, and the pursuit of happiness.

Endnotes

1. William James Dawson, *The Father of a Soldier* (New York: John Lane Company, 1918), pp. 61–62.

2. Michael Blaine, *Co-operation in International Business* (Aldershot: Avebury, 1994), p. 78.

3. Peter Shirlow and Rachel Pain, "The Geographies and Politics of Fear," *Capital & Class*, Issue 80, Summer 2003, p. 15.

4. William Blum, *Rogue State: A Guide to the World's Only Superpower* (Monroe, ME: Common Courage Press, 2000), p.15.

5. John R. Gold and George Revill, "Exploring Landscapes of Marginality, Spectacle and Surveillance," *Capital & Class*, Issue 80, Summer 2003, p. 29.

6. House of Financial Services, U.S. House of Representatives, http://financialservices.house.gov.

7. William Manchester, *American Caesar: Douglas MacArthur* (New York: Dell, 1978), p. 827.

8. I am grateful to Thomas Fleming, the Brit-hating author of *The Illusion of Victory*, for what follows. While I do not even remotely agree that a German victory in World War I would have been preferable, Fleming is surely right on what even the politically correct textbook writers call the "coercive patriotism" of the Wilson period, and which isolationist authors such as Fleming are correct to call a major assault on core American values.

9. Elaine Tyler May, "Echoes of the Cold War: The Aftermath of September 11 at Home," in Mary Didziak (ed.), *September 11 in History: A Watershed Moment?* (Durham, NC: Duke University Press, 2003), p. 49.

10. James Madison, Virginia Convention, May 13, 1798, as cited in Saul Padover (ed.), *The Complete Madison: His Basic Writings* (New York: Harper and Brothers, 1953), p. 339.

11. Peter Shirlow, "Ethno-Sectarianism and the Reproduction of Fear in Belfast," *Capital & Class*, Issue 80, Summer 2003, p. 80.

12. Erica L. Groshen, Bart Hobijn, and Margaret M. McConnell, "U.S. Jobs Gained and Lost through Trade: A Net Measure," *Current Issues in Economics and Finance*, Federal Reserve Bank of New York, Volume 11, Number 8, August 2005, p. 1.

13. Gold and Revill, "Exploring Landscapes of Marginality, Spectacle and Surveillance," p. 37.

14. Barry Rubin, "The Origins of the PLO's Terrorism," Barry Rubin (ed.), *Terrorism and Politics* (Basingstoke: Macmillan, 1991), p. 153.

15. Neil Livingstone, "Proactive Responses to Terrorism: Reprisals, Pre-emption and Retribution," Neil Livingstone and Terrell Arnold (eds.), *Fighting Back: Winning the War Against Terrorism* (Lexington, MA: Lexington Books, 1986), p. 128.

16. Roger Cohen, "U.S. 'Greatest' Rhetoric Alienates Many Abroad," *International Herald Tribune*, September 15, 2004, p. 2.

17. Shoshana Zuboff, *In the Age of the Smart Machine: The Future of Work and Power*, (Oxford: Heinemann, 1988), p. 389.

18. Shirlow, "Ethno-Sectarianism and the Reproduction of Fear in Belfast," p. 83.

19. Richard Hofstadter, *The Paranoid Style in American Politics and Other Essays* (Cambridge, MA: Harvard University Press, 1996).

20. Margaret Chase Smith, "Declaration of Conscience Speech," *Congressional Record*, June 1, 1950.